Just Stories

(that really happened)

While all of these stories are true, some names and identifying details have been changed.

This book may be purchased in bulk for sales promotions, premiums, and fundraisers. Please contact Carole Balawender at facebook.com/pages/juststories for more information.

ISBN: 978-1502439369

For my readers, who are forging
ahead with newfound wisdom

contents

welcome

This book is full of simple, everyday stories about moments in my life that, I realized with hindsight, each brought me an important message. I have included these messages with each story.

For me, some of these moments were meant to savor, and some were just meant to get through. I think of all the moments, good and bad, as "When…" times—for example, "When You Follow Your Dreams…" and "When You Think Things Can't Get Any Worse and You Find Out They Have…"

I hope that by sharing these stories, I will help you recall that you are worthy of all the wonderful things you bring to you. Even the worst of times can bring something good. You just have to notice.

When the "good" arrives, remember to say, "Yes. Thank you! More please."

When the "bad" arrives, remember to say, "This too shall pass."

And no matter what, always remember that you are Spirit in form. Let that Spirit lead you. It knows what to do.

WHEN YOU THINK

THINGS CAN'T GET ANY WORSE

AND YOU FIND OUT

THEY HAVE...

welcome

This book is full of simple, everyday stories about moments in my life that, I realized with hindsight, each brought me an important message. I have included these messages with each story.

For me, some of these moments were meant to savor, and some were just meant to get through. I think of all the moments, good and bad, as "When..." times—for example, "When You Follow Your Dreams..." and "When You Think Things Can't Get Any Worse and You Find Out They Have..."

I hope that by sharing these stories, I will help you recall that you are worthy of all the wonderful things you bring to you. Even the worst of times can bring something good. You just have to notice.

When the "good" arrives, remember to say, "Yes. Thank you! More please."

When the "bad" arrives, remember to say, "This too shall pass."

And no matter what, always remember that you are Spirit in form. Let that Spirit lead you. It knows what to do.

WHEN YOU THINK
THINGS CAN'T GET ANY WORSE
AND YOU FIND OUT
THEY HAVE...

I read only romance novels with happy endings. One of them is by Elizabeth Lowell. The book has a series of quotes that I can laugh at now but that rang so painfully true the year my marriage was ending.

If a man wants a woman and she doesn't want him, it's her fault.
If a woman wants a man and he doesn't want her, it's her fault.
If a man marries the "wrong" woman, it's her fault.
If a woman marries the "wrong" man, it's her fault.

It was these same thoughts that set the stage for the drama that unfolded—drama that began before I consciously knew my ten-year marriage was failing. Each event was a bookend to the beginning and end of its demise.

The drama begins
It was fall. My husband, Rich, and I were just settling into our newly purchased ten acres, which was also home to our newly purchased horse. Rich, who was a talented landscaper, was working on an arbor and waterfall feature. I was working on figuring out what it took to own a horse. In the evenings we would go for a walk with our two dogs down to the end of our road. It was a peaceful place near sunset. Cars on our dead-end road were few and far between. The edge of the gently rising foothills began to our west, and the narrow ridges of deep-red hogbacks were to the north. To the east lay our seven acres of pasture. I was living my dream come true.

The drama began one day that same fall in the late afternoon. I was on my way to get my horse, Thor, fitted for a new saddle. As part of the figuring out what it took to own a horse, I had learned that a saddle must not only fit the rider, it must also fit the horse.

I had left work early that day and was driving my normal route into town. In the glaring sun, a crosswalk light flashed yellow in front of me. I stopped, heard the screeching of tires on pavement, and felt the slam from behind me as I was lurched forward, the seat belt digging into my left shoulder. The rest of my upper body barely missed the steering wheel.

After my heart stopped racing, I stepped out of the car in my riding boots and breeches.

The car behind that had just rear-ended me was not going anywhere but behind a tow truck. The grill now looked to be part of the engine, and the radiator was bent and leaking.

I glanced down at the back of my car and sighed. My Subaru was caved in at the back, but at least it was still drivable.

The door to the car behind me opened. The driver was speaking her apologies before she made it all of the way out of her car.

"I am so sorry," she said. "I couldn't stop in time."

After calling the police, exchanging the necessary information, and explaining to the officer what happened, I called Rich then drove the woman home and continued on to meet the owner of Happy Horse tack shop for the saddle fitting. I was more shook up than injured, or so I thought.

The next day, though, my neck felt like it had been to places that were not part of its normal routine. I waited a day or two to see whether the pain would subside. It remained.

After an exam and x-ray, I was diagnosed with whiplash.

Many months, chiropractor adjustments, doctor visits, and massages later, I was ready to begin to return to a more normal routine. Finally I would get to ride my horse again.

By now it was late summer and time for event number two. One evening, Rich and I returned from an afternoon motorcycle ride along the back roads east of Fort Collins, Colorado. It was a pleasant ride and a pleasant day.

Rich's niece Lindsay from Long Island, New York, was staying with us at the time. We had spent a few long weekends that summer taking her to see the sights of Colorado, Wyoming, and southern Montana. Although Rich and I never tired of the sights and sounds of the mountains, I was pretty sure Lindsay still preferred the sights and sounds of Long Island.

After chatting with Lindsay about our motorcycle ride, Rich left on one of his frequent "ice cream" runs, and I changed into my horseback-riding clothes.

I walked down the dirt-and-gravel driveway to the barn and grabbed Thor's halter, bridle, and saddle. I dropped the saddle onto the railing of the outdoor arena, hung the bridle on the fence post, and headed out into the pasture, the rope halter in hand, to round up Thor. Thor looked up from grazing and headed in my direction. He knew the routine. As soon as we met, I scratched his ears and turned to walk back toward the barn. Thor whinnied in appreciation of the ear scratch and followed me. He never really needed the halter except to keep his head tied to the fence railing so that it stayed raised when being saddled. He preferred to *graze* quietly rather than to *stand* quietly during our saddling routine.

This time the routine didn't go as planned. After placing the halter on Thor's head, but before I had a chance to tie the lead rope to the fence rail, I saw that the lead rope had somehow wrapped itself around my index finger. At that same moment, Thor snapped up his head and almost took the tip of my finger with him. Half of my fingertip was ripped to the bone. I looked down and could see only blood where that half of my fingertip should have been.

I called out Lindsay's name and headed to the house.

"Call Rich," was all I could manage to say. She saw my finger and ran to the phone.

I stood in shock at the kitchen sink, running cold water over my finger, hoping it would slow down the bleeding.

Luckily Rich was already on his way back.

After he returned home, we bandaged my finger to try to stop the bleeding and headed to the emergency room.

At the emergency room, I was led off to be admitted while Rich and Lindsay headed to the waiting room. After answering the series of standard questions, the young man who was checking me in casually said, "I think we can save your finger." It wasn't until then that I cried.

Many stitches later, my fingertip and I were reunited. The prognosis: It would reattach no problem, although it might never be perfectly straight again. A crooked fingertip was much better than a missing one, I thought.

Later that same summer, while my finger and I were still going to physical therapy, another set of words shook my world. The words were simple. "I want a divorce," Rich stated. Those four words said so much more than I was

Just Stories
(that really happened)

CAROLE BALAWENDER

willing to hear. I felt like I was reliving the car accident, only this time it was an emotional slam.

It wasn't until weeks later that I found out Rich had been having an affair. A few of my friends had tried to tell me that they couldn't imagine he would leave unless there was someone else. I couldn't hear them until I found a $300 credit-card charge for a room in a bed and breakfast in Drake, Colorado, outside Rocky Mountain National Park. Rich and I had never stayed there.

Hindsight is 20/20
Looking back, here is what I know now.

It was during the fall of my car accident that Rich had begun his affair. By the time I was in the emergency room with my detached fingertip, Rich had already "detached" himself from our marriage. Rich may have been in the waiting room, but in the truest sense, I was alone in that emergency room— alone with my tears and alone with my pain. One mishap had earmarked the beginning of the affair and another the end of our marriage.

And perhaps because patterns of events often come in threes, yet another mishap earmarked our "official" divorce. This one was in a grocery store parking lot a few days before the official divorce papers were signed. My new car and I were backing out of the parking space at the same time the car behind me was backing out. I heard the crunch before I saw the car. The other driver had done the same. This time the only things harmed were the cars and my attitude. Unbelievable, I thought. What are the chances of that? And my brand new car of only a few days. It was the exclamation point to my self-judgment and self-blame.

Our own below-the-surface thoughts can be so harmful. Our

subconscious knows that something is wrong well before our conscious catches up. In time, I realized that I was literally "beating myself up" for a failing marriage before I was even consciously aware that it was failing.

When "bad" things happen, consider whether you are punishing yourself. Contemplate your thoughts, and change the ones that need changing. If you find that your thoughts smack of self-judgment or self-blame, try shifting them to self-love and self-forgiveness. And, as in my case, if you aren't aware that you are in self-judgment and self-blame but "accidents" are happening, look for the good in your life and be kind to yourself.

Looking back, I also know that redirecting thoughts takes time, practice, and tenacity.

To help me remember, I keep a gratitude journal next to my bed (along with my romance novels). Even on bad days, I stop to contemplate the things for which I am grateful. I believe it is those thoughts that can bring more good, just as thoughts of self-judgment and self-blame can bring the "bad."

pay attention

It was less than two weeks after Rich had left our ten-year marriage and our ten-acre home. He no longer loved me, and, actually, never did. Oh, and by the way, he had wasted ten years of his life with me and couldn't wait to start really living. Those were his parting words.

The torn envelope lay on the chopping block of the kitchen. The image of the $300 Visa charge to the bed and breakfast where Rich and I had never stayed was seared in my mind.

Next in my new role as marital Sherlock came the pages of "business" phone records listing the multiple and daily phone calls to a familiar number that, as it turned out, matched the phone number on the business card of someone who was supposed to have been my friend.

The closing scenes of a bad movie that I just had to rewind.

During the replay, I saw many things.

Revisited actions and behaviors took on a new meaning. There was the long weekend Rich took "alone" on his motorcycle. Looking back, I realized it was at the same time that Pam, his new lover, was riding one of the Colorado Rockies bicycle tours. There was also the argument Rich and I had in the kitchen, about what I don't even remember. Rich's ex-brother-in-law was also there, questioning why Rich was being so mean and telling him to back off.

But it was the actions of others who crossed our paths and what appeared to me at the time to be only happenstance that I see anew now.

The affairs

We had chosen a one-man company to redo the heating system in our home. As a reference, he took us to one of the homes in which he had most recently installed a similar hot-water heating system. During our visit there, we learned that the owner of the house was newly divorced. One day, after nearly completing our home, the still-married contractor brought the newly divorced woman with him on one of his visits to our home. I recall thinking that it was quite unusual, but I was in the middle of a horseback-riding lesson at the time of their arrival and departure. I found out later from the friend who had recommended him that he was having an affair with this woman.

Closer to our own hearts and about the same time, two sets of our married friends were struggling with the discovery of "another man." One marriage lasted, and one did not.

The lost wedding ring

Then there was the lost wedding ring. Rich and I were putting up new fencing on our property. By late afternoon, after removing my work gloves for the nth time, I noticed that my wedding ring was missing.

"Oh my gosh," I cried. "My ring is gone!"

"It's probably in the grass somewhere along the fence," Rich responded. "It's not going to be easy to find."

We searched the tall grasses that ran along the fence line, but to no avail.

"Let's try where we unloaded the fence posts," suggested Rich.

After another lengthy search, a flash of gold caught my eye as it glistened in the low-lying rays of the sun near our driveway. The half-carat diamond was nestled gemstone-down in the dirt.

"Thank goodness!" was all I could manage to say. It had been a stressful several hours, during which I was certain the ring was gone forever.

The wind chimes

But it was the wind chimes that were the most powerful and final symbol of the end of our marriage. Shortly after Rich left, as I was going through belongings to downsize what was left behind, I came across what had been a wedding gift of wind chimes. Quite beautiful really. Our names and the date of our wedding had been engraved on the wooden clapper that hung below the chimes.

That morning, though, when I rediscovered the wind chimes in the drawer of an end table, I remembered that one day not long before Rich had left, the wind had blown fiercely and I had found the engraved wooden clapper split in two: *Rich* on one piece, *Carole* on the other. I had tucked the pieces away with the idea of mending them.

I held the pieces in my hand before discarding them. Some things that are broken just can't be fixed.

We are given the information that we need every day. We just need to pay attention.

you can't always know the big picture

I keep a picture of the horse I used to own in my office. His name is Thor—a mighty name for a small Icelandic. In the photo his ears are lifted in attention. The small white star on his forehead stands out from the fuzz of his chestnut-brown coat. His bleached-blond, Tina-Turner mane is windblown, and his soft brown eyes are looking off into the distance.

I sold Thor this past summer. In our eight years together, Thor taught me a lot of lessons.

One of them is that things aren't always as they appear. Here is Thor's story.

The move
After my divorce from Rich, I moved to higher ground in the foothills of Bellevue, Colorado, and took Thor and my two donkeys, Sonora and Brewster, with me. The new property was eight-tenths of a mile up a sometimes steep and often washboarded dirt road. There were two sometimes-troublesome switchbacks on the way to the house, particularly in the snows of winter and the muds of spring. The property itself was also rugged and steep, but it offered breathtaking views of the red, narrow ridges of the hogbacks to the north and the water and rocky coastline of Horsetooth Reservoir to the east. The city of Fort Collins lay just beyond the reservoir.

The property itself had a small fenced-in area that used to house llamas and would work as a temporary corral for Thor and the donkeys. I would eventually need to fence in most of the property.

Not able to manage the road with a trailer full of animals myself, I asked a friend to help me take the animals and a load of hay to their new home. By late afternoon, the garage was full of hay and the animals were secure, or so I thought, in the corral.

My friend and I went into the house to clean up from the dust and dirt of hauling 50 bales of hay. Within the hour, Thor, Sonora, and Brewster had found an opening in the temporary fencing. We heard the clop of hooves on the dirt road and looked out the window to see Thor and the donkeys heading up the road. My friend and I rounded them up, locked them back in the corral, and mended the fencing.

The great escape

A few days later, already in the rhythm of the new feeding routine, I donned my headlamp, walked out in the darkness of pre-dawn to the garage, grabbed an armful of hay, and headed to the corral to feed the animals. Instead of three four-legged animals glad to see me, I faced a wide-open gate and an empty corral.

Panicked, I scanned the property with my headlamp and then headed back to the house to get the keys and then to the driveway to get the car. I drove down the road in the hopes that even if I couldn't see them, they would see me and make known their presence. It was still so dark that all I could determine was they weren't standing in or along the road between the house and the adjacent Lory State Park. I didn't even want to consider the "what-if" they had gone into the vast park grounds, largely inaccessible by car.

Distraught, I called a friend who had horses in the valley to the north, not far from where I lived. Erica helped to assuage my fears of never finding them or finding them injured and suggested I wait until the light of day to continue my search.

As I waited impatiently for the sun to rise, I thought of the property where Rich and I had lived at the time of our divorce. After Rich left, I had remained there for almost a year. During that time, I had mistakenly left the gate open one morning. More than eight hours later, when I came home from work, Thor, Sonora, and Brewster were all standing outside the gate and outside the barn door awaiting my return. Or so I like to think.

"Why do they keep leaving the new place when they'd 'waited' for me to come home at our old property?", "Where have they gone?" and "How long have they been gone?" were the thoughts that plagued my mind until first light that morning.

At dawn, I headed down the road again. This time, I found the donkeys grazing on a nearby neighbor's golf-course green. Happy to see me, they brayed right outside my neighbor's window. I would apologize later, I thought as I drove back home with the car and returned with their halters to lead them back to the corral. I secured the gate with extra wire and headed out in search of Thor.

It turned out that Thor had decided to go to even greener pastures a mile down the road in Lory State Park, a place where we had frequently ridden before moving to the new property. Luckily, during his visit to Lory, Thor followed a person kind enough to lead him to a corral at the bottom of my road, which is where I found him and the kind person

14

who explained what had happened.

Needless to say, our new home wasn't working out for everyone. I wasn't sure anymore that I had it in me to take care of a new home and three large animals that didn't seem to want to stick around. After the donkeys' escapade at the neighbor's house, I also finally considered that braying donkeys on the ten acres where we used to live were a lot less intrusive than braying donkeys on the three acres where we now lived, especially if they ever found their way back to my neighbor's golf green.

Bessie

I had some things to reconsider. Oh, and there was also the business of "Bessie" the tractor to deal with. Bessie had originally come with the ten-acre property where Rich and I had lived. Before I left that property, I had arranged to sell the tractor to help pay for the fence that I had planned to build at the new place.

I had promised to sell Bessie to a man named Kenny, who lived on 30 acres in Wellington, a town about 30 minutes northeast. I had left Bessie at my former property until Kenny could pick her up. A few days after the animals' great escape, he and I met so he could look over Bessie and we could finalize the deal.

"What did you do with your donkeys?" Kenny asked before we even discussed the tractor.

I gave him an earful about their wanderlust. Kenny responded with an offer to take them. "I love donkeys," he replied. "Not many people appreciate them." They would be company and protection for his calves.

I had seen Sonora's protective instincts when she had fended off one of our dogs from Brewster, who was her son. After seeing the hooves of a donkey in action, I knew they were not creatures to be messed with. Although Sonora could have killed our dog, she merely rolled him, and he whimpered away unharmed. Although it was only a warning, it was one he would never forget. It appeared that Kenny really did know about donkeys.

I hadn't even thought to try to find the donkeys a new home, but now that it came up, it seemed like a good solution. The donkeys would have a purpose. I could tell that Kenny was a man who meant what he said and would take good care of them.

We negotiated the price of the tractor-and-donkey package deal. Kenny agreed, wrote the check, and arranged to pick up the tractor and the donkeys at a later date.

Although I was relieved to have found a new home for the donkeys, I was also sad. Standing outside my previous home, I looked out at the corral and thought of our morning routines. Thor, Sonora, and Brewster would all line up at the gate before I let them out to their pasture. Each would stop and rest his or her head on my stomach for an ear scratch and head rub before heading out. In addition to that ritual, being greeted every morning by braying donkeys is pretty special, especially when you imagine it is because they are so happy to see you.

So much had changed since the days of our morning routine. Each day was a new awakening to just how much. Keeping the animals at the new property no longer seemed like a good idea. The ruggedness of the property, which I had seen only as beauty when I decided to buy it, did not make it the best place for grazing. Although they would miss Thor, the donkeys would be much better off on 30 acres of pasture. And my new neighbors would have peace.

Thor's move

Letting go of the donkeys was difficult enough. I simply could not part with Thor. We had bonded like only a horse and rider can. We had grown together through many trainers and lessons, including dressage, eventing, and western riding. We had joined the Back Country Horsemen of Colorado and had gone on trail rides at every opportunity. We even ran together. And throughout all of those lessons and rides, it was Thor who was helping to mend my aching heart.

Although I would miss having him around every day, boarding Thor was now an option and the best thing to do. I could not afford to board three animals, but one was doable. And my Mr. Social horse would not be happy alone. Boarding him would ensure that he had horse pals.

Thor's first boarding place was a few miles down the road from where I had moved. During his first year of boarding, I continued to see him almost every day. We rode most every weekend. But as the months passed, life happened, work became more demanding, and I saw Thor less and less. It takes time to be a horsewoman, and I no longer had the time.

After two years, I started searching for a new place to keep him where he would be ridden and get in the people time that seemed so important to him. Through a friend, I found someone interested in boarding and occasionally riding him just down the road from where he was currently boarded.

Horse heaven on earth

Thor's new home was horse heaven on earth: beautiful green pastures, a running stream, three other horses, and two very caring and thoughtful people to take care of him. Those caring people, Steph and John, had planned to occasionally ride Thor while one of their horses was healing from an injury. Unfortunately, Thor spent more time eating the lush grass than being ridden. Before a year was up, his once fit and trim figure looked to be heading into the obesity category. Being fat is not healthy for any animal. If Thor continued to gain weight, he would eventually be in danger of laminitis. A horse suffering from laminitis experiences a decrease in blood flow to the laminae, which is attached to the horse's hooves. The end result is extreme pain, a horse that cannot even walk, and, if allowed to get severe enough, death.

What happened to horse heaven on earth?

To save Thor, I moved him to dryland pasture north and east of town—pretty darned barren, lots of wind, and one other horse. Although he still had people time in the form of two beautiful young girls, ages 11 and six, who brushed and rode him, he had lost his lush grass all-you-can-eat buffet and found himself at a Weight Watcher's camp for horses.

But now that Thor was even farther away, I saw him even less than the monthly visits to Steph and John's place.

The ad

I finally decided that the best thing for Thor was to sell him. He needed a job, someone to whom he could really belong, and a home.

After mentioning my plans to my friend Erica, she recommended posting an ad on an Internet site called Dream

Horse. I searched the site to determine whether there were any Icelandic horses for sale. I found a few, but none of them came close to Thor.

For the ad I had to write a description of Thor. But describing him in 150 words or less was not an easy task. In the contemplating of those 150 words came the memories.

The first words that came were *smart as a whip*. During our many riding lessons, Thor was so smart that he quickly learned the trainer and trainee routine. Here is how it was supposed to go (at least for the more difficult maneuvers that required a demonstration): The trainer rides the horse to show the trainee how to cue the horse and what the end result should look like. The trainee gets on the horse, tries the cue, and hopes for the same results. In Thor's case, when the trainee (that was me) mounted him, Thor often did what he knew we wanted, whether I cued him correctly or not—not good for a rider trying to learn to ride, but very endearing nonetheless. Thanks to his original owner, he also knew just about every Parelli cue invented. (Parelli is a well-known set of horse-training methods and cues.) In fact, Thor knew many more of them than I even knew to try.

During our eventing lessons, eager-to-please Thor would try to jump over almost anything on the ground, including the trot poles. (Eventing is a competition that involves cross-country rides and jumping over stationary objects, such as logs and walls.) Trot poles were used during training to enable the horse to get into the correct trotting rhythm to prepare for a jump. It took a while for my trainer to get Thor to understand that he should only trot over trot poles. It reminded me of our dog Oakley, who, after learning to fetch the newspaper, brought us all the newspapers in the neighborhood. In fact, Thor was kind of like a very large dog.

During our runs, if it was on our ten acres, I didn't even need a rope or halter to lead him along. We would play a game in which we would run side-by-side and I would stop suddenly. He would miraculously stop the instant I did. I'd run again and he'd be right there with me, ready to stop on a dime. I am not sure which of us enjoyed that game more.

Entertaining was another word that came to mind as I composed the ad, but I wasn't sure how to explain that in the ad. I decided to save those stories for follow-up phone conversations with prospective buyers. I don't know of any other horse that could do Thor's apple or carrot trick, which Thor's original owner had shown me. When I held a horse treat behind his front legs, Thor would bow his head and reach for it like a true gentleman.

Mischievous was another word that would fit. Thor and Brewster had somehow learned a Houdini magic trick. To this day, I am not sure how they did it, but almost every time I blanketed them, Thor and Brewster's blankets would be lying out in the pasture before the day's end.

Playful fit as well. I'll never forget the day that my first trainer canceled our riding lesson because of the wind. It is difficult to hear in the wind, and some horses get more frisky when it is windy. I had only owned Thor a month or two. Still green to riding, I was considering saddling him up anyway to go for a short ride. When I looked out the window to see whether Thor was close to the house or out to pasture, I saw the donkeys run past, followed by Thor, who was chasing them around the house. I lost count of how many laps they ran, but decided maybe my trainer had the right idea after all.

Next was *perfect trail companion*. On the trail, Thor was fearless and sure-footed. Nothing appeared to faze him. While other horses shied away from large objects or fast-flowing streams, Thor kept right on going. If there was any hesitation, it was on my part. If I fell off, which happened infrequently, he would stop and wait for me to get back on.

Without a doubt, Thor was the most friendly and people-oriented horse on the planet. In fact, Thor was such a people horse, I often wondered if he thought he was a four-legged person. The acreage where we used to live had a front gate that enabled me to enclose all ten acres. Thor would often come up to the front porch of the house to visit as if waiting to be invited inside. (He had actually been inside the home of his original owner.) He enjoyed people company so much, he had even stuck his head in the cab of a running Bobcat one day to say "hi" to Rich, who was inside.

When it came to ranking his temperament, thinking of the running Bobcat incident, I selected the highest score.

On the ground with other horses, Thor was also quite possessive. As soon as I went near any other horse, even his horse buddies, he would run them off. I couldn't decide if that was a good or bad quality, so I left that part out to also save for a follow-up conversation.

And, finally, Thor and I had spent four days training with the famous horse trainer Buck Brannaman. He was the trainer that *The Horse Whisperer* movie was about. I definitely needed a mention of our time with Buck in the ad.

Here is what I wrote:

Friendly, extremely cute, and smart-as-a-whip 13-year-old gelding. Thor loves people and is very calm. He is trained in Parelli and other natural horsemanship methods. He has attended multiple dressage clinics, and has been in a four-day workshop with Buck Brannaman. He has had beginning training for eventing, so he knows how to move through trot poles. Thor loves to go for runs and is very playful. He is an excellent horse for trail riding and will follow you without a lead in the round pen. He has been ridden both English and Western and is an easy keeper, with excellent hooves and teeth. He is calm enough to lead into your home (I have a picture to prove it) and has stuck his head in the cab of running Bobcat machinery. He comes to you so you do not have to "catch" him and stands for the vet and ferrier.

The big picture completed

After placing the ad on Dream Horse, I had many inquiries but only one person who was serious enough to see him. At that time, Thor was still too large and the potential buyer could not ride him comfortably. I believe that was my test run to get used to the idea of really letting him go. It was not a great feeling, but I decided there is truth to the adage that if you love someone (or a horse), you need to set him free. If it was meant to be, we would find a good home for him and in time I would hold onto the memories and learn to let go of the sadness over missing him and knowing that he would no longer be around.

Thanks to the property owner's diligence and caring, within the year, Thor had shed his extra pounds and returned to his fit and trim self. He was ready to be seriously ridden again.

Two months almost to the day after his one-year anniversary at his "what-happened-to-horse-heaven-on-earth" lodgings, the call came. It was our first trainer, asking about Thor for a client. She had seen the ad and remembered Thor. I knew that this time Thor would be sold. When a trainer recommends a horse to you, you listen. And as this first trainer knew, Thor was a pretty special guy.

I returned the call and arranged for them to meet Thor without me. I was really busy at work at the time, and I wasn't sure I wanted to be there. Seeing my previous trainer Lynn would bring back many memories, some of which I was trying to forget. After exchanging several phone calls with Lynn's riding student, Jane, I knew Jane would be perfect. She was caring, thoughtful, happy, and she was definitely interested. She also lived with her husband on 35 acres in Livermore, northwest of Fort Collins, and had another horse and two donkeys. Thor would be right at home there.

It turned out that all five-foot two of Jane was one big smile and heart. We decided to give it a one-month trial period. If Thor or Jane were not happy, I would take him back. "What a perfect idea!" I thought, although I knew in my heart Thor was gone. He was too darned lovable and smart to bring back. It turned out I was right.

Looking back

I always wondered what Thor thought of his last move before I sold him, if horses even think of such things. Here is what I tell myself when I think of it, especially when things aren't the way I think they should be.

You just can't always know the big picture.

From Thor's perspective, he went from an all-you-can-eat smorgasbord of lush grass to a Weight Watcher's desert. But just as we can't always know the why or big picture of things, Thor had no idea he was being saved from the severe pain of potential laminitis.

What we need to know is that it all works out for the best, even when we can't imagine how it will ever get better. In the end, thanks to the wonderful people who owned that barren and windy spot, Thor became the handsome and fit horse that was under all that fat and fuzz. And because he was fit and ever-so-handsome, he found a new home with some kind and caring people.

Today Thor's life is full of limited time in lush, green pastures, daily brushings, groundwork, walks, rides, donkeys, horse pals, and all kinds of love and attention. And it took at least seven paint-by-number brushstrokes (my move, two escapes, selling a tractor and two donkeys, and three boarding places) to complete the picture.

Thor's story is worth remembering.

WHEN YOU THINK IT IS
YOUR HORSE'S FAULT...

Maybe your horse knows more than you think

Being the social creature he is, Thor never met a horse (or donkey) he didn't like, with one notable exception (more on that in a moment).

I first learned of the extent of Thor's gregarious nature the day he arrived at the property where Rich and I lived at the time. We already owned the pair of donkeys, a mother and son. While preparing for Thor's arrival, I learned that it is a good idea to separate large animals for a day to give them time to check each other out and to see how they will get along.

Not wanting any injured animals, the day Thor arrived we put him in the corral and kept the donkeys in the pasture, with a fence between them. They each walked along the fence line, sometimes pointing their noses at each other, sometimes pointing their noses in the air, sometimes walking or running in parallel, and sometimes saying whatever horses and donkeys say to each other when they first meet.

A couple of hours later, the sky in the distance turned from blue to indigo. The storm that was brewing off in the horizon was moving in quickly. I could smell the coming rain.

After discussing our options, Rich and I decided to open the pasture gate to give everyone access to the barn. Sonora, the mother donkey, was the most timid. After I opened the gate, she decided to let her son, Brewster, and Thor figure things out while she stood off in the distance. Thor and Brewster only seemed interested in playing and chasing each other around. Feeling settled, we left for the house.

When the rains began, we were no longer able to see the animals. Too curious to wait for the storm to pass, Rich and I headed out to our three-stall barn. I opened the barn door to find three pairs of eyes looking out at us over the same stall gate. Thor, Sonora, and Brewster had somehow managed to crowd together into the same stall. They appeared to be perfectly content and quite happy to be together. "So much for that worry," I thought.

The first time I was with Thor when he met a horse he didn't know was also my first time riding Thor without his original owner. The horse was named Blackhawk. I had met him and his owner, Pam, in the neighborhood where Rich and I used to live. Pam would run with her donkeys and Blackhawk through the neighborhood. In fact, it was Pam who had inspired me to later get donkeys and to run with them and with Thor.

At this time, I still didn't own Thor but was riding him to keep him exercised for a friend. Pam, an experienced rider, also knew Thor's owner at the time. Pam and I decided to ride together down the road from where Thor lived. At the end of the road was a trail that followed the ridgeline of the foothills and crossed over the other side to Horsetooth Reservoir. It was a beautiful spot and a well-used trail close to town.

The next weekend, Pam and I trailered her horse to where Thor was living. I went in the back of the property to saddle Thor and brought him out to the front property to meet Blackhawk. They sniffed at each other, whinnied, and were ready to hit the trail. We only rode for a couple of hours, but everyone got along fine that day.

Many months later, after Rich and I had moved to the ten acres and after I had bought Thor, Pam and I talked of bringing Blackhawk to board at our property. Blackhawk would get more room to roam than he had on Pam and her husband's smaller lot, and Rich and I would have a second horse so that he and I could ride together. By this time, Pam, Rich, Pam's husband, Tim, and I had all come to know each other. It seemed like a win-win for everyone involved.

The day Pam and Tim trailered Blackhawk to our property, we never thought to begin by separating Blackhawk and Thor. After all, they had already met and had gotten along fine.

Pam led Blackhawk out of the trailer and through our open gate. As soon as Blackhawk was released into the pasture, hooves began to fly. Thor reared up on his back legs in a way I had only seen in movies. Blackhawk returned the gesture. Horse screams filled the interludes between the clashing of hooves.

Trying not to panic, and hoping they wouldn't kill each other, we did the only thing we could do, which was to wait it out.

When things settled down, the horses were separated and examined. How each remained unharmed was more than I could comprehend. Needless to say, the plan needed to change.

What was that all about?
I had never seen or heard of Thor doing such a thing. It was perplexing and disconcerting. I made a note to stick to the initial separation rule on our property, no matter how well Thor knew the guest horse.

In our eight years together, Thor met and rode with at least 50 other horses, including the horses in the numerous horse clinics we attended. The aggressiveness he displayed toward Blackhawk never happened again.

Looking back on that day and its timing, I now believe that Thor was looking out for me in more ways than one. I will never know for sure what Thor was thinking or why he did what he did. But perhaps Thor understood something that I discovered too late.

It wasn't until a full year later that I realized that on the day Thor and Blackhawk had it out, Pam and Rich were already having an affair. The affair had started after Pam and I had ridden together the first time but before Pam brought Blackhawk to our property.

Of course, having Blackhawk on our property would have been a perfect excuse for Pam to spend time at our place with or without me there.

Perhaps Thor was trying to warn me that something was wrong in the only way he knew how. Maybe it was his way of saying that Blackhawk wasn't really his friend, just as Pam really wasn't mine.

Don't be so quick to blame others

If you own a horse or have only ridden one, you have probably been faced with at least one instance in which the horse was doing one thing and you were thinking it should be doing something else.

I was tested by my horse, Thor, in more ways than I can count. He knew when I passed and when I didn't. That is the wonderful thing about horses: They see right through you. If you need lessons in consistency, balance, patience, focus, being present, or remaining steadfast, take horseback-riding lessons.

And when you find yourself blaming the horse for a mishap, think again. One of my last lessons on Thor was much more than a riding lesson.

Although we ran together quite often, I hadn't ridden Thor much, if at all, for most of the winter when he moved to Steph and John's just before the spring thaw. (This was the "horse heaven on earth" place.) After the spring thaw, I decided it was time to get back in the saddle.

The first time we rode together in the fields of horse heaven, we did more ground work than riding. It was a beautiful spring evening. When I drove up into Steph and John's driveway, Thor and his two horse buddies (Steph and John's horses) came up to the gate to greet me.

I grabbed his halter, which was hanging on the fence, and walked toward the gate to get him. Thor did his usual "she

belongs to me routine" and ran off the other horses when I opened the gate to the pasture and stepped inside.

I led Thor across the driveway and yard into the round pen, closed the gate, and went to retrieve his saddle and bridle back at my horse trailer, which was also staying with Steph and John. After Thor was saddled and bridled, I used a lunge line, which is a long, thin pole with a rope on the end, to guide him to run some circles around the perimeter of the pen.

Here's how it goes: When I raise the lunge line and point it in a particular direction, Thor trots around the circle in the same direction the lunge line is pointing. When I change the direction of the line, Thor also changes direction and continues to trot around the pen. When I lower the lunge line, Thor stops to face me. I bow my head, which is his signal to return to me.

That evening after the lunging routine, we did a few laps, turns, and stops together, Thor "glued" to my right shoulder without any cues and without a rope. This meant he was paying attention to me and was ready to ride.

I grabbed the reins of his bridle, placed my left foot in the stirrup and swung my right leg around to the other side. I was riding in my English saddle, which was more lightweight. It felt good to be seated on Thor again. I missed riding him.

We started out in a walk across the round pen. Although my plan was to go straight ahead, Thor kept moving to the left as if following a diagonal. I pressed my left leg against him to nudge him to the right, hoping he would straighten, to no avail. I also locked my gaze straight ahead, as if to add emphasis to my leg commands. I had been told repeatedly that if you look where you want to go, the horse will follow. But Thor seemed to be ignoring my cues and insisted on walking a diagonal.

"C'mon, Thor. Go straight!" I commanded. I might as well have been talking to the fence railing. In response to the "C'mon," which is the only one of the four words he knew besides his name, Thor picked up the pace.

Frustrated, I cued him to trot. But even following the perimeter of the round pen, he kept cutting to the left.

This is not fun, I thought. And based on experience, I knew it would do no good to keep trying to get Thor to stay straight, as it would just be frustrating for both of us. I asked him to halt, and I dismounted.

I grabbed the lunge line to lunge Thor in a trot, to at least get him exercised. Thor's third time around the pen, Steph walked up to the gate to say "hi."

We struck up a conversation about Thor. Steph mentioned what a good boy Thor was and how everyone enjoyed having him around, including her two horses. "They seem to be inseparable," she said.

Normally, I would have agreed with the Thor being a good boy part, but not tonight. Fine, I thought. He's such a schmoozer. She must be giving him carrots or apples. Sure enough, as the conversation continued, Steph mentioned how much Thor seemed to appreciate carrots.

"I was thinking of bringing Timalin out for some lessons on Thor," Steph continued. "Timalin is a horse trainer who is also a horse whisperer. She can read a horse on the first meeting."

"That sounds like a great idea. Let me know how the lessons go and what she says about him," I requested. I knew it would be a while before I would be back. Perhaps Timalin could explain the diagonal stride to Steph before I rode him again.

It was a few weeks before I was able to return to Steph and John's to ride Thor. I repeated the warm-up followed by riding routine, with the same results. Once in the saddle, when I asked Thor to walk out, he walked his diagonal path yet again. I pushed my leg against him to try to nudge him over. He insisted on moving to the left. When I tried using my right leg farther back to cue him to correct his course, his response was to turn in a circle.

Argggghhh. He was actually doing the right thing by circling, I thought. What the heck. A lesson from Timalin was sounding better and better. For now, it was back to ground work. Just then, Steph came out to see us.

Although Steph had not yet had a lesson on Thor, she reported that Timalin had been out and had met Thor. She also said that Timalin was impressed with Thor. She thought he was very friendly and very smart.

Maybe if Timalin watches me ride him, Thor will behave because he is being watched, I thought. Thor liked being the center of attention and responded to praise. Perhaps he would try to show off for Timalin.

Steph gave me Timalin's contact information, which I immediately transferred to my phone. I called Timalin the next day and explained the unwanted diagonal routine. I arranged for a lesson the following week.

The lesson fell on another beautiful evening. I had Thor already saddled and ready to go in the round pen before

Timalin arrived. When she pulled up in her pick-up truck and stepped out, Thor and I watched her approach. I liked her before she even spoke. She was smiling, had an easy stride in her blue jeans and riding boots, and seemed very approachable and down to earth.

Timalin introduced herself and asked about my riding experience. I explained that I had owned Thor for about seven years and that we had taken lots of lessons in dressage, eventing, and western riding. I also explained how Thor knew many more Parelli cues than I did. I reminded her of my diagonal dilemma, explaining that I had not ridden Thor for most of the past year.

"Get on him, and let's see you walk out across the round pen and then ride him at a walk a few times around," she instructed. Thor took off on a diagonal, while I kept trying to straighten him out.

"See how he is moving in a diagonal instead of facing straight ahead?" I asked.

"Shift your weight in the saddle to your right," she said in response. "And go around again."

I shifted in the saddle to the right. Thor straightened out as well, heading out straight ahead this time. We walked the perimeter of the round pen perfectly.

"What happened?!" I exclaimed.

"Thor was just trying to hold you up," she explained. "You were leaning too far over to the left. He kept moving over because it felt to him like you were about to fall off. You must be tighter on one side. I can show you some stretches."

I couldn't believe it. Thor had simply been trying to protect me.

I was too busy being in awe of Timalin and Thor to spend any time being embarrassed, although I should have been. Instead, I was filled with appreciation for what a wonderful horse Thor kept turning out to be.

"Wow! How cool is that?" I said.

"He's a good guy," Timalin confirmed and left me to my aha moment before continuing our lesson.

Humbled, I now try to relate that lesson to other areas of my life...especially when I am certain something can't possibly be my fault. "Don't be so quick to blame others" was my real riding lesson that day. When something isn't going as I think it should, I know I need to look at myself first.

WHEN YOU DON'T KNOW

WHETHER TO LAUGH OR CRY...

sometimes it's best to laugh

In the house where Rich and I lived outside Fort Collins, we dug two water wells on the property during the course of the one year that we lived there. The first well went dry. The second one turned out to be full of very muddy water. Not good. What made it especially bad was that it was winter and, since Rich had recently left our house and our marriage, I was alone.

Luckily, the property had a large cistern, which is an underground water storage tank. Lined with cement and covered with a removable metal lid, the cistern was buried near the driveway on the west side of the house. I just had to make sure it didn't become empty, because an empty cistern meant no showers, no washing dishes, no flushing toilets, and no water for me or for the animals to drink

When we lived there together, hauling water simply meant that Rich drove into Fort Collins every week in the red Ford F-350 pickup, filled the 200-gallon plastic water tank that fit in the bed of the truck, drove it back to the house, and used a hose to transfer the water from the plastic tank to the cistern. Simple, right?

It was simple until winter came and Rich left with his new lover for the beaches of Mexico. While Rich was basking in the sun, I was hauling water in subzero temperatures (18 below, to be exact). I had put off getting water as long as possible, in hopes the weather would warm up, but the below-zero temperatures were here to stay.

37

I slipped into my Carhartt overalls and jacket, pulled on my Sorel boots, grabbed my purse and cell phone, and headed out to the garage.

After climbing into the cab, I found the ignition and turned the key. I heard the whimper of an engine that did not plan to start. I tried again, this time holding the key in place. Only the whimper again, followed by silence. It seemed the truck's diesel engine would not start in the freezing temperatures, even though it was parked in our insulated garage.

I reached over to grab the cell phone and dialed Rich's number. .

"Why are you calling me?" was his greeting.

"It just happens to be 18 below zero, the truck won't start, and I need water. I need to know where the engine heater is and how to use it," I snapped.

I don't recall Rich's instructions, but I followed them. A few hours later, the truck, the water tank, and I were headed to town. So far so good.

Then the good part ended.

Once in town, I pulled up next to the water station and stepped out of the truck into the frosty air. I grabbed the metal rod attached to the water hose that I would use to fill my plastic water tank.

It did not reach.

Climbing back into the truck, I backed up a bit and pulled closer. Hopping out again, I grabbed the hose. It still would not reach, but it was oh-so-close.

What did I do wrong? I thought. I am good person. Why am I here in the middle of a deepfreeze, while Rich is basking in the sun in Mexico? And why is he gone during the coldest time I have ever experienced while living on this property?

I watched the steam of my breath as I begged the universe to help me park the truck perfectly this time.

When I realigned the truck yet again, it reached the hose and water spigot with room to spare.

Thank you universe!

I climbed into the bed of the truck and wrapped both hands around the plastic lid to the water tank in the truck bed. My hands moved in a twisting motion in an attempt to open it, but the lid did not budge. I took off my gloves to try barehanded, in case the gloves were slipping. Still the lid didn't budge. I used all of the strength that my 112-pound body could muster and tried again. The lid was frozen shut. I slipped my already-numb fingers back into my gloves.

The betrayals were lining up in my head. First were Rich's lies about the reasons for the divorce, then the discovery of an affair, followed by the discovery that the person he was having an affair with was supposedly a friend, followed by more lies and the trip to Mexico. It was the very same trip that Rich and I had planned to take together—except Rich had known even during the planning that his traveling companion would be Pam.

I could have fallen apart right then, but I didn't. I redirected my thoughts to the reality at hand. This was not a time for tears or hysteria. Getting water was not an optional matter. I could save the losing it for later if I chose to do so.

If I wasn't already so angry, I am sure I would have seen the humor in my situation a lot sooner.

Well, I certainly did this water-getting thing backwards, I

realized. I could have saved myself a lot of time and trouble if I had only tried to open the lid first, before I came to town.

I laid my head on the frozen water tank, and I laughed. It was the kind of laugh that a bystander, had there been one, could have mistaken for hysteria. My body repeatedly heaved against the water tank, barely making a sound except for the occasional gasp for air.

It took only a few minutes of laughter in the subzero cold for my head to clear. Time to use the hair dryer, I thought. There was an outlet in the garage—the very same outlet I had used to heat the engine. I would use the hair dryer to thaw the frozen lid until it opened, then I would leave the lid open until I returned with the water tank full. I headed back home. If only everything in life were so simple.

sometimes you just need to cry

This is a very short story. But it encompassed many years of my life. It was the day I sold Thor.

I left the house in plenty of time that morning so I could spend an extra hour or two with Thor before our final goodbye. Although I had already shed many tears over the course of the week, I knew it was all good. He was going to a wonderful home.

I had no plans for what we would do together during our last couple of hours together. I just knew I needed my Mr. Thor time to get the preliminary goodbyes out of my system before his new owners arrived to take him away.

The sun peaked in and out of the clouds as I drove east towards the town of Wellington, where Thor had lived the past year. As I got closer to the property, the wind became relentless. I had forgotten about the wind that seems to blow, if nowhere else, always at Thor's current boarding place. We would definitely be staying close to the shed and out of the wind.

As I was driving up the long dirt driveway to the property, I saw Thor grazing off in the distance, his mane following the direction of the wind. Grazing was Thor's favorite pastime.

Shannon, who owned the property, was heading out to run an errand. We stopped to chat for a few minutes, our cars side by side. She mentioned how she and her family would miss having Thor around. I nodded in reply and smiled. I steered the conversation to the weather and a thank you for being so kind to Thor.

I was grateful that Thor and I would be alone.

I grabbed my sunglasses before stepping out of the car in case I needed the cover up for any stray tears.

As I walked toward the pasture, Thor looked up and headed my way. We no longer had a routine, but he never failed to seem happy to see me.

"Hi, Mr. Thor," was all I could say. I wrapped my arms around his neck. Thor whinnied in response and nuzzled closer. He seemed to appreciate my hug as the warmth of the tears that had made their way down my cheeks moistened the chestnut fur of his nose.

I unwrapped my arms from his neck and walked toward the shed. Thor followed. He picked up his pace, but I still walked slowly.

Once in the protection of the shed, I grabbed Thor's brush and currycomb. He was pretty dusty from the wind, and his mane could always use a combing. It wasn't dreadlocks, exactly, but it was definitely coarse and unruly. I brushed every inch of him more than once, and occasionally threw in some hugs and an ear scratch for good measure.

Next, because standing still is not my nature, I grabbed Thor's halter out of the shed and placed it over his head. We headed back out into the wind and went for a walk in the pasture. I wasn't in the mood or dressed for running, and it was too windy to ride. But despite the wind, going for a walk seemed like the right thing to do. Movement always seemed to keep my mind from "running." It probably wasn't the smartest order of events, but I was just doing what I thought to do next. During our walk, I told Thor about my day and explained why he was going to another home. I told him I loved him and thanked him for our time together. Who knows what he heard, maybe just the wind, but he stayed close and fell into the rhythm of our walk.

Next came my "sit with Thor time." In the evenings where we used to live, I would often go into the corral near the barn and just sit with the animals. Being curious and wanting more than the company of donkeys, Thor would come over and just stand there, his nose close to mine. Today we did our sit time back at the shed. Instead of being sad, I was grateful for the time we had had together. How many horses will hang out with their owners for "sit time"?, I asked myself. A few nuzzles later, the horse inspector arrived to fill out the bill of sale papers.

By the time the inspector walked down towards the pasture, my clothes were brushed clean and I stood to meet him. Shortly after I signed the bill of sale papers, Thor's new owners arrived. I positioned my sunglasses over my eyes, just in case, and mumbled, "Here goes," to Thor and the wind.

Thor whinnied as the pickup truck pulling a trailer that I am sure smelled of other horses stopped near the gate where Thor and I were standing. Jane, her husband, and a neighbor stepped out of the truck and waved in greeting.

"Sorry we are late," Jane said.

"Isn't he a handsome guy," said her husband.

After introductions, we talked about the day, the bill of sale, and Thor. Meanwhile, Thor got a lot of rubs and scratches. Soon Jane asked if I would lead Thor into the trailer.

"Of course," I replied.

I grabbed the lead rope, led Thor out past the squeaky metal gate, and walked toward the open trailer. Thor followed as usual, his head keeping the rhythm of our walk. At the door of the trailer, he hesitated and stopped, both front feet firmly planted.

I tugged gently on the lead rope to circle around and try again. "It's OK, Mr. Thor," I said soothingly. We circled around in the dust of the driveway. This time I sensed Thor's hesitation and kept circling around again. It was a larger trailer than the one we had. However, Thor was used to getting into different trailers and had never hesitated in the past.

Three's a charm, as they say. This time around, I stepped up and into the trailer and Thor followed. I led him to the front, dropped the rope for the new owners to tie him in, and started walking out. Thor, being a small guy, could also turn around in most any trailer. As soon as I turned and stepped forward, Thor turned to follow me back out.

I stopped, grabbed the lead rope, tied it loosely around the metal slats of the trailer, and headed for the door without looking back. Jane's husband took my cue and passed by me to keep Thor inside. The tears were flowing freely now. I had no words but apology, trying to explain between sobs that I had come early to get those tears out of my system. If Thor hadn't turned around to follow me out of the trailer, I assured them, I would have been just fine.

Jane understood. She and her husband and neighbor let me cry in private as they closed up the trailer with Thor inside and got into the cab of their truck. When I was ready, Jane handed me the check. "You can come visit him anytime," she assured me. "We will take good care of him."

I thanked them, gave Thor one more nose rub through the trailer's metal slots, and waved goodbye.

I knew then that all of my tears were about so much more than Thor. He was my last stronghold on the life I had loved and dreamed of. I cried for all the letting go…letting go of sharing the ranch lifestyle with someone; letting go of the dream of loving someone who loved you in return; and letting go of the dream of being a horsewoman. Some dreams are not meant to last a lifetime.

I said my goodbyes to more than Thor that day. And in the grieving, sometimes you just need to cry.

WHEN YOU ARE TRYING TO

SETTLE INTO A NEW LIFE...

sometimes you need to move through feeling unsettled

When Rich decided to leave our marriage, I was determined to stay on the acreage. I loved the life there, the animals, and the property—well, minus the hauling water part, but the water eventually cleared in the second well. That part seemed taken care of, at least.

However, the house was in shambles at the time, quite the symbol for what seemed to be my life. Rich and I had redone the heating system, but the walls and ceilings throughout the house had been torn open to accommodate the new ductwork, and they weren't yet repaired. The barn also needed work.

Weeks later, the patched drywall and repainting still weren't enough to cover up the memories that lived there. Despite my struggle to find normalcy in a life that no longer felt normal, I was still determined to stay.

A few of my friends had just the ticket. One evening after dinner at my house (I loved to entertain), they conspired in kindness.

"I'll help with the dishes," said my friend Teresa as she started gathering the plates and leftovers from the dining room table.

"Thanks! We can just put them all in the dishwasher," I explained. "It shouldn't take long."

Teresa and I headed to the kitchen. Randy, Teresa's husband, and Cynthia stayed behind.

Standing at the sink with Teresa, I thought I heard the shuffle of socks on the wood floor.

Teresa pointed to something out the window over the kitchen sink and kept on talking. I am sure at the time it seemed interesting, important, or both.

About half an hour later, the food put away and the dishwasher loaded, I hung the dishtowel to dry.

Teresa and I were still on a conversational roll. This time our attention was focused on a horse carving that had been a gift from a friend and that was hanging over the door in the kitchen that led to the front porch. Out of the corner of my eye, I saw Randy and Cynthia carrying my long, narrow table out of the adjoining room.

"What are Randy and Cynthia up to?" I asked.

"Just rearranging some furniture," Teresa responded.

I smiled and walked out to the dining room. The brown leather couch that used to face the woodburning stove now faced the window that framed the foothills. On cold nights, Rich and I used to sit on that couch, watching and enjoying the warmth of the fire. Now when I sat on the couch I would look out the window toward the foothills. Nice, I thought.

The overstuffed leather chair that I would drape myself over to read was also on the opposite side of the room from where it had been. Rather than having my back against the wall, when I sat in this chair now, I would be facing yet another window.

The antique rocking chair was moved from the sitting room and into the living room. More room for company to gather, I thought.

The long, rustic table that used to be in the living room

behind the couch replaced the rocking chair. It was now against the wall in the sitting room that led up to the master bedroom upstairs. Not only was it moved, but on its surface Randy had arranged some small river rocks into a wavy pattern intermingled with sand dollars collected from a trip to the west coast. The rocks and sand dollars had been hidden at the bottom of a small glass vase. Randy's design traced the long edge of the table and pointed in the direction of the stairs to the bedroom. It was a simple and beautiful work of art.

"I didn't know you were such an artist!" I exclaimed to Randy. "It is beautiful!"

My heart was touched to the point of tears. Good tears.

In that one short evening, with the help of my friends, the house had begun its transformation from a place of only memories to a place in which to start my new life. It had begun to feel like a new home in which I could settle. The rearrangement of furniture had triggered a rearrangement in my perspective.

Inspired, I imagined new paint in vibrant colors.

"I see cats living here," said Randy as we all lounged on the rearranged furniture in the living room.

At the time, I wasn't so sure I wanted the extra responsibility of even more animals in addition to my two donkeys, a horse, and five chickens.

But by the next day, I had become a woman with a mission, determined to complete what my friends had begun. Within a few weeks, the bedroom, bathroom, and two downstairs sitting rooms changed from whites and browns to strategically placed walls of deep rust, mauve, burgundy, and yellow, all with crisp white trim. A new loveseat, throw, and a couple of new pictures also made their way to my home. And thanks to Randy's diligence and assistance, two very loving kittens also became part of my new life and animal family. It's my place now, I thought.

All it took was a kickstart from a few kind and thoughtful friends. I am eternally grateful for their thoughtfulness, knowing, inspiration, and friendship.

When you are troubled, reach out to whomever reaches back. Someone is always there for you. And if you know someone going through difficult times, don't forget him or her during the aftermath. Sometimes, settling back into normalcy when nothing seems to be the same goes easier with a little help from good friends.

WHEN YOU KNOW

SOMETHING IS RIGHT FOR YOU...

watch for the "wow!" factor

I have made plenty of mistakes in my life that have taken me off course. But somehow I always manage to get back on track. And sometimes I just know when something is right for me.

Another thing about me that I have finally come to terms with is that I rarely make logical decisions. Even big ones. From the outside, I look impulsive, and sometimes I am. But when I have a knowing, it starts out as a solid decision.

In hindsight, I can see that one of the things I've always seemed to have a knowing about is where to live. It has taken four houses to get there, but looking back on the chain of events that led to the purchase of each home, I have much more faith in my intuition than I did when that chain of events started. Each purchase has a remarkable story, starting with the ten-acre ranch where I lived with Rich for the last year of our marriage.

House number one
How Rich and I ended up purchasing our small ranch was due, in part, to a horse. He was a roper, and he was fast. (A roper is a horse that can make quick turns to enable the rider to "rope" another animal.)

It was early spring. I was in an indoor arena taking group horseback-riding lessons that were recommended to me by a friend. This same friend told me about some acreage at the base of the Poudre Canyon that was for sale by owner. The Poudre Canyon is a scenic east-west route through

Colorado's Rocky Mountains northwest of Fort Collins. Based on my friend's description, the acreage seemed a perfect fit. Rich and I had just started talking about moving to a house with more land. At the time, we lived on a half-acre just outside Fort Collins.

It turned out that the owner of the acreage my friend had mentioned was at the same riding lesson as I was that day. It also turned out that during that lesson my horse spooked at some snow falling off the roof of the arena. As the snow landed with a loud thud against metal, my horse took an abrupt 90-degree turn, while I continued moving in a straight line, landing in the dirt quite some distance away.

Another thing you need to know about me is that I am the most fearless when I am learning something new and oblivious to danger. This was well before I had even met Thor or spent any time riding a horse. I dusted myself off, climbed back on, and attempted to appear calm under my instructor's order to settle my horse down.

Later, when I called about the acreage and met the owner, Kit, there, she recognized me from the riding lesson. She mentioned that she was impressed by the way I handled myself after the fall. We bonded as horsewomen, even though I was as green as snot and she was an exceptional rider. I also bonded with the property, which included a three-stall barn, an outdoor arena, a fenced in corral, and a three-bedroom stucco house with a balcony off the master bedroom

I brought Rich with me for a follow-up visit. After a trip home to discuss the pros and cons of the property and how much we wanted to pay, we met Kit and her husband, Bill, a few days later and struck a deal that was contingent upon selling our current home.

Not long afterward, Kit and Bill received another offer on their property. We had to commit without the contingency or back out. After another lengthy discussion, we committed.

As the closing on our new home neared, no one had made an offer on the house where we were still living. Rich and I were both nervous about the thought of making two house payments. It would be a bigger stretch for us financially than we wanted to make. Yet I so wanted to live on the acreage I had already come to think of as "ours."

The chain of events required for us to sell our existing house and take ownership of the new property all seemed to happen overnight. The timing of things was definitely down to the wire. Within less than a month of our closing date, our real-estate agent sold not only our house, but also the house of the people who wanted to buy our home. Wow!

I often look for the "wow!" factor in things that happen to me to reinforce that something is meant to be. I didn't know I needed to live on the new property at the time, but I certainly knew that I wanted to. The acreage and the life there, down to our chickens, was a dream come true for me. I am grateful to this day that I was able to live there.

And who would believe that I would meet the owner right before our negotiations and that our real-estate agent would be able to sell two houses within two weeks to make it all fall into place? And this was not during a hot real-estate market.

Wow, indeed!

On to house number two…
I never planned on leaving that ten-acre property, but then I also never planned on getting a divorce. Two years later, when I decided to leave, another pretty remarkable story unfolded.

This house was the one on three acres in the foothills. It could have been my dream home if I had ever thought to dream that big. A skylight in the bedroom, a balcony, two fireplaces, vaulted ceilings, a humungous bathtub, a bookcase on one wall, a gigantic walk-in closet, and double doors to the master bedroom. Best of all, windows everywhere, of all different shapes and sizes, and all with fantastic views. Some overlooked the nearby reservoir and its rocky coastline, and others opened onto views of the narrow, red ridges of the hogbacks to the north. Outside, the two-car garage had an apartment off the back and an outbuilding with sliding doors and a view toward the reservoir. It even had a small fenced-in area for my horse and two donkeys.

"They" say never to make big decisions shortly after a divorce. Perhaps it was not a wise decision for me to move there. But I can tell you this: Although I bid quite a bit lower than the asking price and insisted that the appliances be included with the house, the owners accepted my offer. I later learned that they had turned down another offer. Although I am sure there was a logical explanation for it, the fact that it happened, no matter the reason, was enough confirmation that I was making the right move.

But the "wow!" factors continued to happen. Next, there were the blue doors to the master bedroom. I had purchased a framed photograph of blue doors the year before at a local gallery. It caught my eye one evening when Rich and I were walking in the older section of Fort Collins, close to where we lived when we were first married.

The photograph looked like a setting in Paris, France. The blue doors had a long, wrought-iron latch that slid across both doors with an old-fashioned lock hanging from the end to secure it. The door was also tastefully weathered. In the photograph, it was framed by tiers of flowers on one side and a whitewashed and worn wooden chair on the other.

As it happened, the blue doors in the picture looked exactly like the blue doors to the master bedroom in this house. An artist friend of mine insisted they were one and the same. I insisted she had to be wrong. It turned out she was right. The owners knew the photographer, who had purchased the doors after taking the photograph, and had subsequently sold them to the homeowners.

The final "wow!" factor occurred when I asked the real-estate agent to find out who owned the land to the north of this house. I wanted to make sure no one would build there, ruining the views. Her inquiry revealed that the land to the north was actually part of the three acres that went with the house.

So there you have it. I lived in that home for three years.

On to house number three…
After selling the ten-acre property to Rich, I decided to buy another property as an investment. This time the home was in the older section of Fort Collins, known as Old Town. Old Town Fort Collins is the heart of the city, full of very large and very old trees and old homes full of character.

When my real-estate agent, Corinne, and I arrived at the property, I looked past the waist-high wooden picket fence, with its copper-capped posts, that surrounded the front yard. What I saw could have been on the cover of *Better Homes and Gardens* magazine. It looked like a rainbow had swept through, leaving every color imaginable in its wake. Brilliant orange poppies; white and pink azaleas; deep red, pink, and white roses; orange and yellow daylilies; a pastel palette of iris; deep-pink echinacea; white daisies; a lilac bush; baby's breath; and other kinds of groundcover and flowers I could not name filled that yard.

"Let's wait in the gazebo until Ann is ready for you to see inside the house," suggested Corinne.

I closed my gaping mouth to answer, "Sure..." as she led me through the side gate to the back yard. This yard was filled with yet more splashes of color. What I remember most were the towering giant pink, red, and white cosmos that swayed in the breeze, the trellis of purple clematis, and yet more rosebushes. Much of the back yard was also covered in the delicate white baby's breath groundcover.

Corinne opened the door to the gazebo that was tucked away beside a huge tree on the far side of the yard. I followed her inside. After sitting quietly in the gazebo for a few moments, I knew I wanted to buy the place without even going inside the house. It felt special and well cared for.

It wasn't long before the homeowner, Ann, came out to greet us. I liked her the moment I saw her as well. It was her warm smile and eyes that had envisioned such a place, I thought. And it was those weathered hands that had toiled to turn that vision into such a magical reality. I was honored to meet her.

The house was also warm, inviting, and well-kept. I liked everything about it. Another plus was that the house and the garage were clad in lovely and low-maintenance brick.

But, one small glitch: It turned out that the house was already under contract for the asking price. Another real-estate agent had offered to buy it. Well, at least I have good taste in houses, I thought.

No big deal. I didn't have to have that house or any other house, really. But then came the final "wow!" factor for this house. When Corinne talked to the agent who already had the house under contract, he offered to back out. The house was mine.

House number four…
The home where I now live is also in Old Town Fort Collins. And the story of how I came to own it is equally remarkable. A friend of mine named Warrell had been looking at houses in Old Town and had made an offer on this one that was refused. She then decided to remodel her current home and stay there instead.

Not long after, I was walking in Old Town with a different friend. We stopped at the house, really just to pass the time. I knew it was empty, as Warrell had mentioned that the owners had already moved to the Carolinas. Although I had never been inside, while standing on the front porch I had an overwhelming feeling that I needed to live there. I felt at home and at peace. I knew the neighbors directly across the street and one house over, and I had lived around the corner and down the street, only a few blocks away. Perhaps it was the familiarity that was a comfort to me.

The house itself was stucco, with a wooden front porch and a swing. Lovely, but I was also drawn to the yard. The front yard was small but full of foliage and flowers, most of subtle and darker colors including clematis, ornamental pampas grass, rosebushes, the incredibly fragrant Carol Mackie daphne bushes, coralbells, many flowers I couldn't name, and a towering elm tree. The driveway was lined with lilacs. In the back yard were hostas, hydrangea, roses, a purple butterfly bush, and a plum tree. The house bordered an alley, so there was some distance between the house and the neighbors to the north. The south side was buffered by the yard, which actually filled more of the south side of the house than the back.

Accustomed to my decisions based on gut feelings, the friend who was with me listened as I told her my spur-of-the-moment plan and did not question my decision.

Next, I contacted my real-estate agent and made an offer. My offer was accepted, my loan was approved, and here I am.

Many "wow!" pieces had to fall in place for this house to become mine as well. I intended to keep my home in the foothills and rent it out. But I had to show income on that property for my new loan to be approved. Although the rent I was asking for the foothills house was not cheap, the move would be at the end of December, and the windy road to the house was washboarded and steep, the house was rented almost as soon as I placed the ad.

Next, both of the houses needed to appraise for a certain value. They did, despite the fact that this was during the recession, when real estate values were still on their downhill slide.

Third, I was being investigated for fraud. I had inquired about a refinance with a couple of financial companies. The one I did not select never closed out my paperwork. It actually took a call from my real-estate agent to the CEO of the mortgage company to straighten out that one. The fact that he was even willing to speak to her still amazes me to this day.

Then there is the part where I had until five in the afternoon on the day the movers came to close on the house before the contract would be null and void. With most of my furniture already inside the new place, the paperwork, the title company representative, and the mortgage broker all arrived just before four. We were signing papers on the bench in the yard while the movers were bringing in the last pieces of furniture. Well, except for the furniture that wouldn't fit down the narrow stairs to the lower level. Even that worked out after a quick phone call. My new tenant offered to buy that furniture and move it back.

And did I mention the winter storm that passed through the next day, after my two cats, my many large plants, and I were already happily moved in?

Lordy, is all I can say. You can come to your own conclusions. But I am sticking to mine. It was all meant to be. With all the synchronicities, how could it possibly be otherwise?

When you get a feeling that something is right for you, listen and watch for the "wow!" factors to follow.

WHEN YOU FOLLOW YOUR DREAMS...

My wanderlust began with a trip to Toronto at the age of 17. By the time I was 18, I had been to the coast of Maine and to Montreal and Quebec. I had also traveled to England and Ireland. I returned from the U.K. a seasoned traveler, an experienced hitchhiker, and a connoisseur of picturesque and magnificent scenery.

My next trip, and the subject of this story, was closer to home, which at the time was Detroit, Michigan. It started with a friend's calendar and a picture of the Maroon Bells, in Aspen, Colorado. Unlike the rolling green hills of Ireland, these mountains were jagged, steep, and snow-kissed. It looked to be a magnificent place. I wanted desperately to go there.

My friend, Dan, was an amateur filmmaker. His house was full of images. The calendar with the photo of the Maroon Bells hung in the hallway leading to his office. Although Dan had an appreciation for beautiful places, a trip to the Maroon Bells was not on his bucket list. He was a city guy through and through. It was the images and people of Detroit, where we lived, that captured his interest and attention. Meanwhile, I was slowly becoming a wanna-be country girl with a yearning to spend more time in nature.

No problem. I had other friends, one of whom had been to Colorado. His name was Gary. We had wanderlust in common. We had met in the neighborhood bar, which is where I went to find him to tell him about the Maroon Bells. He told me about his friend Duff, who had recently moved to Steamboat Springs, Colorado. Carless, Duff had just returned to his parent's home in Birmingham, Michigan, a Detroit suburb, so he could ship his belongings to Steamboat Springs before returning to his new home there. According to Gary, Duff was planning to hitchhike from Detroit back to Steamboat in the not-too-distant future.

Steamboat Springs seemed close enough to Aspen to me. At least both places were in Colorado.

Suggesting that Duff and I meet, Gary drove me early one morning to the home of Duff's parents. After answering the door, Duff returned to the couch where he had been sleeping. We followed. It was not until Gary spoke the words "I'd like you to meet Carole" that Duff realized Gary had brought someone with him and rolled over to face us. There I stood, all five-foot six of me, 110 pounds, beach-blonde hair, bronze skin, and a body the shape of a strand of linguine. There Duff lay, well-built, thick dirty-blond hair, closely shaven beard, and trimmed mustache—the epitome of Mr. Outdoorsman. I instantly felt safe and secure and crossed my fingers that he would agree to let me go with him.

Gary explained my plans to see the Maroon Bells and my desire to hitchhike to Steamboat. Duff's version of the rest of the story of our meeting goes like this: "I saw this beautiful blonde with a fetching smile. When I found out she wanted to hitchhike with me to Steamboat, I broke my vow to never hitchhike with a woman." And there you have it. My trip to Colorado was on.

The journey begins
Two days later Gary dropped us off on Interstate 94 at Telegraph Road, barely outside the suburbs of Detroit. I was loaded down with a backpack full of clothes and camping

gear. Duff had two packs, one of clothes and one of books that had been too heavy to ship to Colorado.

I was more excited about seeing the mountains of Colorado than worried about the perils of hitchhiking. In my experience, hitchhiking had been only a positive adventure. True to my experiences, our route from I-94 to I-69 and then to I-70 was positive but uneventful until we entered St. Louis.

On the west end of the city and late into the night, I was still excited about the trip, while Duff, a seasoned hitchhiker, was falling asleep on his feet. After a handful of passing cars, few and far between, Duff instructed me to "wake him up when I got a ride" as he headed off to take a nap along the highway. I tentatively raised my thumb in the headlights of each passing car. I realized that night that I was much braver in the light of day and with my hitchhiking partner at my side.

Six hours later, we still had no ride. Soon after swapping places and stating, "Here. Let me show you how it's done," Duff, true to his word, landed us a ride in a rusted-out and dented Volkswagen Beetle. That driver took us all the way to Denver, Colorado, where we spent the night in a motel, the driver in one room and Duff and I in another.

My bravado went down a notch that evening while my esteem for Duff went up multiple notches. Shortly after we checked in to the motel, a knock on our room door was followed by a muffled outside conversation between Duff and our driver. It seemed that the driver wanted to know whether he could "have me" after Duff was done. I was aghast at the news, but Duff assured me that he had defended my honor and set the man straight. Nevertheless, I did not sleep well that night. The thought of that man in the same building was more than disconcerting.

After his spurned advances, our driver left before we awoke in the morning, taking Duff's forgotten pack of books with him. Despite the loss of Duff's books, I couldn't have been more grateful that the man was gone.

Our next stop was Winter Park, Colorado, a mountain town where Duff's parents owned a condominium. Showered, much more well-rested and another hitchhiked ride later, we were in what was the beginnings of Ski Time Square at the base of Steamboat Springs' ski resort.

I spent the next couple of days exploring the town of Steamboat Springs, buying additional camping supplies and food, and repacking for the rest of my trip. My two days in Steamboat also included a hike to the top of the ski mountain, Mt. Werner, a warm up to hiking the Maroon Bells, which lay 200 windy mountain miles to the south.

Maroon Bells or bust
Determined to see the Maroon Bells up close and personal, I said my goodbyes to Duff, polished my thumb, and hit the road. I don't recall all the places I passed to get to the Maroon Bells nor the number of rides it took. I do recall my first glimpse of the Maroon Bells. They were spectacular, just like the picture, and I was ecstatic.

My initial ecstasy was followed by desperation as, after being dropped off at a campsite along Maroon Creek Road with the Maroon Bells still in the distance, I stared bleakly at the pieces of my borrowed tent. Although I bonded with the woods of Michigan, I was still a city girl who had no idea how to put those pieces together.

I lined up the tent poles, wishing they were color-coded to identify which pieces went together and where. I then unrolled the tent. My no-brainer activities completed, I stared at the line of poles and started to arrange and connect them in a variety of combinations, none of which resulted in an upright tent.

A young man in the next campsite must have heard or noticed my sigh of dismay. Or perhaps it was the repeated clanging of poles. No matter, being neighborly, he stopped by and offered to help. Once again I was facing Mr. Outdoorsman. This time he had dark brown hair, was clean-cut, clean-shaven, and dressed in khaki. I am certain my next sigh was one of relief.

After the tent was set, so was I. My gracious neighbor had also offered to accompany me the next day on my quest to visit the Maroon Bells. The thought of having a companion, who knew the ropes and the area, seemed like a great idea to me. Morning couldn't come soon enough.

The following few days were full of first experiences. My first backpacking trip, my first "real" campfire, my first time cooking on a camp stove, my first taste of camping food, and my first dream come true.

Sometimes being naive is a good thing, and sometimes not. Who knows what would have occurred if that young man had not crossed my path. But he had. And I got to see the Maroon Bells as I dreamed I would.

The detour
With the Maroon Bells checked off my bucket list, I set off to visit a former boyfriend, Michael, who lived in Phoenix, Arizona. My plans also included stopping in Sedona along the way to buy turquoise jewelry. I had learned that Sedona, an artist's mecca, was famous for its beautiful turquoise at the time.

But as "they" say, even the best-laid plans don't always work out exactly as planned, especially in the hitchhiker's universe. Instead of heading to Sedona, what happened next was a detour to the Grand Canyon, followed by a visit to San Diego.

Not far outside of Aspen, where my backpacking partner had dropped me off, I got a ride from a softspoken, kindhearted Jewish man, who had a full head of red hair and a beard to match. His name was Nehemiah. Nehemiah was on his way to the Grand Canyon and then to San Diego, where he lived. The Grand Canyon and the Pacific Ocean were two more firsts that sounded like great places to add to my bucket list. I can't tell you exactly how, but I knew with every cell of my being that Nehemiah was a "good guy." I asked to tag along. He graciously agreed.

At the Grand Canyon, I saw yet another aspect of spectacular and the true meaning of grand. I also saw more colors of dirt and rocks that I had ever imagined. And on that trip, I learned what it meant to break in hiking boots. That was a first I could have done without. The Maroon Bells hike was a piece of cake compared to the relentless switchbacks of the Grand Canyon. Time on the beach with no shoes was the perfect next stop.

Once in San Diego, I was enthralled with the city, its restaurants, its beaches, and its residents. Despite my relatively landlocked childhood, I also had an inexplicable affinity for whales and was enamored with the idea of seeing one. While on the beach, I relentlessly scanned the horizon for a spout, fluke, or fin, but to no avail.

Before I headed back toward Arizona, Nehemiah also took me on a side trip to Tijuana, just so I could say I'd made it to Mexico. We only spent a few hours there. The things I remember most are the marimba music, the vivid colors, and the never-ending shops. Thanks to Nehemiah, I was more than safe and saw places I had never even thought to dream of going.

Encounter with an Arizona angel
Hitchhiking from the West Coast back to Arizona, I met many other characters.

I recall a ride in the back of a Volkswagen with a full-grown, black Newfoundland, an elderly rancher who offered to come back and get me for a roll around in the hay if I didn't get a ride, a scar-faced Arizona state trooper who gave me a ticket for hitchhiking, and a traveling salesman who was a guardian angel in disguise.

That traveling salesman picked me up on some deserted road that I, wanting neither a roll in the hay nor a night in jail, had opted to walk after my back-to-back encounters with the rancher and the state trooper. As far as I knew, the road I was on eventually reached Sedona.

It was early afternoon when I began my walk down that deserted highway. It was hot and it was dusty. But it still looked a lot better than what I had left behind. I also thought to myself that I could camp along the road if I didn't make it as far as Sedona that day.

I had been walking only a short time when a car sped by, leaving a wake of dust in its path. In the vicinity of that wake of dust, I heard the screech of slamming breaks and saw that same car going in reverse almost as quickly as it had been going forward.

The driver emerged, not your Mr. Outdoorsman type but instead a well-dressed Mr. Salesman type, who let loose a long lecture about whether I had lost my mind and by the way what was I doing on that deserted road alone and oh was I running away from home.

I stared into the row of shirts that lined the backseat of his car and took a deep breath as I contemplated where to begin my response. I decided that describing my desire to buy turquoise jewelry in Sedona and then to visit a friend in Phoenix would be as good a start as any.

As it turned out, my guardian angel in disguise not only took me to Sedona but to every jewelry store he thought was worth visiting. Thank goodness there were only three of them. He not only knew every store but every storeowner. And he knew turquoise jewelry. I was mesmerized by all of my choices and a bit overwhelmed. At store number three, I ending up buying a large oval ring with a turquoise stone embedded in swirls of silver. It met his "quality" approval as well as the constraints of my pocketbook.

We spent the night in separate rooms in a motel in Sedona with a plan for the morning. The traveling salesman would drive me back to the highway, and I would have a sign in hand that read "Phoenix." I made the sign from the remains of a box and markers borrowed from the motel's front office.

In the morning, after driving me back to the highway, my guardian angel actually waited to make sure I had a ride all the way to Phoenix. The sign had worked. My signal was a thumbs up and a nod to ensure him that the car that stopped would take me to Phoenix, although he still got out of his car to meet and approve of the occupants of the car I was about to climb into.

My roundabout journey back home…
One final detail I've neglected to mention was that I had no plan for how, after Phoenix, I would get back home to Detroit. That detail also took care of itself a few days after I reached Phoenix, with one phone message from Duff. (I had given him Michael's phone number.) Duff had discovered

that a couple of guys, one of whom he worked with, were driving from Steamboat to the East Coast and were more than willing to take the detour to drive me to my doorstep back home in Detroit.

By the time I was ready to leave Phoenix, I was more than comfortable hitchhiking back to Steamboat alone and was excited to get there so I could tell Duff about all of my adventures. The trip was a series of rides in a variety of semi trucks. It was also fairly uneventful, except for my last ride, which took me into the town of Steamboat Springs. Looking out the window of the trucker's cab on my final ride to Steamboat, who should I see on the roadside trying to hitch a ride into Steamboat but Duff. Keep in mind, these were the days before cell phones. At the mercy of my thumb and passing drivers, I had no idea which day or time I would arrive back in Steamboat. The chances of us being on the road in the same place at the same time seemed minimal to none. The trucker graciously stopped for him when I explained that Duff was my friend. The expression on Duff's face when he opened the cab door was priceless.

And here we are at the end of this story. I made it back from Steamboat Springs to Detroit safe and sound, and oh by the way, with only one day to spare before classes started for my fall semester.

Please know that I am not suggesting that women gallivant across the country alone, especially these days. Perhaps it was the fact that, although I was 19, I looked about 13 that kept me safe. I like to believe that I had help from the universe all along the way, including at least six guardian angels, counting Duff and the two young men who drove me back home.

At the time, I did not know I'd be taken care of. I just knew

I wanted to see the Maroon Bells. It is only with hindsight that I now know that I always have assistance, especially to help my dreams come true. I believe that we all have a set of "guardian angels" or soul friends who are here to assist us. So why not take the risk to follow your dreams, too?

amazing things happen

Here is the part of the book where I admit that I have been married not once, but twice.

I met my first husband at Colorado State University, where I was a teaching assistant in the photojournalism lab. I worked in the darkroom, back in the day when such things were common. I was responsible for teaching journalism students darkroom techniques, as well as assisting them in selecting and arranging a series of photographs to tell a compelling story.

I was sitting at my desk in the classroom outside the darkroom, looking over some photographs, when Don walked in. I looked up to face six-foot, two inches of what I considered to be a very attractive man: blue eyes that twinkled, sun-kissed brown hair and mustache, a physique that demanded admiration, and a smile that was all charm.

Not wanting to ogle, I immediately looked away. Looking up again, I composed myself, attempted a charming smile in return, and was all ears to find out why such a man was standing in my classroom. When I learned he was there to visit a friend, I casually bolted towards the darkroom to retrieve his friend. I stayed there, hiding in the shadows until I knew Don was gone. Men that good-looking made me nervous.

Despite my attempts to hide, the universe had other ideas. Our paths crossed again. This time, off campus. After striking up a conversation, Don commented on the fact that I had cut my hair. How he could have possibly remembered what I looked like, let alone the details of the length of my hair, was beyond me. I was a goner. He asked me out. I went. Within a year we were married.

We partied. I stopped. He didn't. We divorced.

Of course, no marriage is really that simple. And no matter the reason, separating from someone you have been with for seven years is still painful. Thanks to Don, I had experienced many outdoor adventures. Now those adventures would once again have to be on my own—at least until I was ready to trust my heart to someone again. My next relationship, I vowed, would start out with more reasons than physical attraction and the opportunity for adventure. "Someone I could grow with" was one of the new items on my list.

After the divorce was final, I swore off men for a year, focused on me, and followed a dream to Hawaii. It wasn't just going to Hawaii that was a dream come true. I went as an Earthwatch volunteer to work with dolphins.

Earthwatch is a program that combines volunteer travel opportunities with scientific research expeditions to protect the planet and its species. I had learned of the Earthwatch program while surfing the web in search of a place to just get away—away from the memories and away from the Colorado home where Don and I had lived and now I lived alone.

I wasn't really able to concentrate on much of anything at the time. Taking time off work from my technical writing job was a good thing. Luckily, I was able to take a month's leave of absence.

According to the website, as an Earthwatch volunteer I would be working with Dr. Louis M. Herman, who was featured in *National Geographic* and who was studying dolphin sensory perception, cognition, and communication.

Working with dolphins and a trip to Hawaii sounded like the perfect getaway. I would be helping a worthwhile cause in a place I had wanted to go ever since I'd returned from New Zealand twelve years earlier.

Oahu - the island of upgrades
I arrived in Hawaii two days early so that I could spend some time on the famous beaches of Waikiki on the island of Oahu, where I would be working.

For my first two nights, I had reserved a less-expensive, lower-level room at one of the hotels on Waikiki beach. The rest of my time on Oahu, I would be staying in the dorms on the university campus.

I arrived at the front desk of my hotel all smiles, anxious to lounge on the beach and play in the ocean. After welcoming me to Oahu, the clerk causally announced that I was being upgraded at no extra charge to an ocean-front room on the top floor. I graciously accepted the offer but waited until I boarded the elevator to clap my hands and exclaim, "Yes!" to no one in particular.

When I entered my upgraded room, the view that awaited me through the sliding doors to my balcony was an expansive sea of blue that eventually met the horizon—much better than the grains of sand that would have been at eye level from my original accommodations.

I stood on my balcony, taking in the simplicity of the view and the soothing sounds of the gently tumbling waves along the coastline that mingled with the muffled sounds of laughter and conversation on the beach below.

Those first two days were filled with basking in the sun, water sports, and thoughts of my dissolved marriage. My ex-husband was from Long Island. Also an ex-lifeguard, he had been an adrenaline and water sports junkie. Our life together had been full of water adventures, including white-water kayaking, sea kayaking, and white-water rafting. On the plus side, the ocean held many great memories. On the down side, thoughts of the ocean were often accompanied by thoughts of Don.

I escaped many of my thoughts by focusing on activities that demanded my concentration. The hotel had every water toy you could imagine, including boogie boards, windsurfers, and inflatable kayaks. I tried them all.

When I needed rest, basking in the gentle sun of Waikiki beach was also much more comforting than the harsh sun of Colorado. Its warmth seemed to permeate to my soul.

Still, waves of loneliness also permeated my soul as I lay on my beach towel in the midst of all the other beach towels that blanketed the beach. While married, I had become accustomed to spending time alone. Don, who was a rafting guide during part of our marriage, had often been away from home in the summer. I went along on the rafting trips when I could, but I was still used to spending weekends on my own. This alone time was different. I was alone in the midst of the crowds of people who filled the beach.

Although I felt lonely, I wasn't really interested in meeting any new people on the trip. I was moving ever inward, deciding who I would be for the next phase of my life. How much of my life had been Don's and how much of all that adventure had been me was a question I could not answer. For now, I knew that my connection to nature would remain. As a result, I couldn't wait to meet the dolphins, which would be part of my new world for the next four weeks.

When it was time to leave the hotel, the clerk at the

front desk of the hotel called for a taxi to drive me to the university campus. I waited outside in the shade with my single piece of luggage. The shade felt refreshing after two days of sun and saltwater, both of which had already begun to streak my already bleach-blonde hair. My skin had also soaked up the sun and was now bronze. I was beginning to feel a part of the island. At least in looks, I might have passed for a surfer dudette.

As my thoughts turned to dolphins, an all-black limousine taxi pulled up and stopped in front of me. I peered inside, waiting for the driver to step out and verify that he was at the right place before I climbed in. Yes, confirmed the driver, the limousine taxi was for me.

This was another first that was duly noted. To me, the limo interior was reminiscent of the expansiveness of the Grand Canyon. Yet as I settled into the leather seat, rather than feeling small, I was feeling quite full of myself. The universe seemed to be sending me a "time to upgrade" message. I was going to need to play the part. I was starting to look quite forward to it.

The dolphins
Once on campus, I settled into my dorm room. It reminded my of my 25 x 58-inch beach towel. A small twin bed, desk, lamp, and single wooden chair filled the room. But no matter, I wouldn't be spending a lot of time there. The campus, on the other hand, seemed immense and oh so tropical. Even the ground itself was green.

The next morning, the routine began. I was to stop by the cafeteria for breakfast and to pick up my box lunch for the day, then hop on the bus that would take us to the research center every morning.

The first day at the center, a short woman with tight black curls, dark skin, a warm smile, and a clipboard in hand stood in bare feet to face us. After taking "roll call," she explained our data-collecting responsibilities and how they related to the dolphin communication and cognitive research to date.

She turned to lead us through the facilities. We followed. What appeared to be water toys of all different colors, shapes, and sizes were strewn over the wet concrete floor. The main criterion appeared to be something that would float.

Once outside, we saw three dolphins gliding in circles just under the surface of the water in the pool below. Ladders, platforms, and stations of flip-up images of simple black-and-white shapes lined the perimeter of the concrete pool.

At the end of the tour and orientation, it was time to officially meet the dolphins. Our leader asked for a volunteer without explaining what we were volunteering for. No matter, I immediately raised my hand and stepped forward. I was instructed to stand on one of the platforms alongside the pool and reach out my hand over the water. As if on cue, a dolphin leapt out of the water, blunt nose to lowered palm, and "kissed" my hand. "Do you believe that?" I exclaimed to the assistants on either side of me. New memories were starting to gently push aside the old ones. I knew I was in the right place.

Maui: the island of the humpback whale
On my weekends off, I took a plane to other islands. The first was Maui. It had whales. After landing on the island and picking up my rental car, I headed toward the bamboo forest on the opposite end of the island to meet up for a hike with a newfound friend who was also on the Earthwatch team.

Preparing for the rather lengthy drive ahead, I opened the map, turned on the radio, and settled in. About 20 minutes from the airport, the road met the ocean. I stared ahead, out across the water and toward the horizon, my thoughts full of anticipation of hiking the bamboo forest.

What happened next was one of the most unbelievable moments of my life. A humpback whale emerged from the water and breached clear above the surface no farther than 20 yards in front of me. Rivulets of water gleamed off its 50 feet of jet-black body, followed by the explosion of water as it resubmerged. OMG. Thank goodness no one was behind me as I slammed on the brakes and exclaimed to no one, "Did you see that!" Pulling over, I looked around for other cars. No one else was nearby.

Not wanting to be late to meet my friend, I continued driving, this time reflecting on what had happened rather than on what was to come. As part of that reflection, I thought of the first time I had seen a humpback up close and personal. I was with Don, on our honeymoon. We had planned a sea-kayaking trip to Alaska. I had picked the place, Tonawek Narrows, in the hopes of seeing humpbacks. That dream had also come true as a humpback surfaced right next to our kayak while we paddled in the cerulean blue water.

My first humpback sighting was a gift I had long tucked away in my heart. Now both scenes were tucked away, but this new memory was mine alone. The ache in at least one place in my heart was beginning to slowly fade away.

Time to cross whale-watching off my list for this weekend.

How my directionally challenged mind and I ever made it to the bamboo forest trailhead is a miracle in itself as

I followed the twisting and winding roads of the island. But make it I did, in time to meet my friend. And oh by the way, the bamboo forest was everything I imagined and more. Although our conversation began with my story of the whale, my Earthwatch friend and I eventually eased into the rhythm of the hike under the canopy of Jack-and-the-beanstalk bamboo and the spray of its infamous waterfalls, which poured out of the lush green mountainside, one 400 feet high.

Kauai: the island of emerald green
My second island was Kauai. My to-do list on this island included a Zodiac tour of the Na Pali coast. Another OMG.

When I landed at the airport, true to my routine, I headed to the rental-car counter. A small red convertible was waiting for me. Before leaving my parking space, I had the top down and felt the sun warm against my skin as I smiled toward the sky. The firsts were starting to get hard to track.

When I arrived at the tour office to board the Zodiac, I learned there had been storms for several weeks, preventing any tours until that very morning. Ocean storms and an inflatable rubber raft with a motor attached would not be a good combination. Gratitude, gratitude, gratitude.

Although the Zodiac ride was choppy, I managed to keep my mouth agape and my eyes glued to the coastline. "Spectacular" took on a new meaning and so did the color green. Every view took my breath away. Cliffs of a deep, unfathomable green jutted straight up out of the ocean. Waterfalls spilled down the ravines that intermittently carved out the mountainside. Although I have not seen any of the Seven Wonders of the World, for me the Na Pali coast should be added as Wonder number eight.

Yet another memory was tucked away in my heart, gently pushing aside the old ones.

The Big Island: the island of fire
Third was the Big Island. This time my dream was to see the active volcano. After arriving in Volcanoes National Park, I discovered that if you wanted to get really close to the active part of the volcano, you needed to take a helicopter tour. The tours launched from Hilo, quite some distance away. I found the nearest phone booth, made a phone call to the number I had been given, and booked the last seat on the last tour of the day. It was a mad dash in the rental car to the other side of the island, and then, poof, my camera and I were boarding the helicopter.

I was the last person to book the flight, but it turns out these tours don't offer first come, first served seating. Instead, it's about balance. Because I was the smallest person, I was seated in the front of the helicopter, next to the pilot, and surrounded by what I assumed to be clear plexiglass, in front of, beside, and below me. Gratitude and excitement beyond measure filled every inch of that helicopter even before we left the ground.

On the way to the volcano, valleys and mountains of lush green, green, and more green filled the helicopter windshield and floor that surrounded me. There was so much to take in as the helicopter sped toward the volcano. I was torn between capturing the unobstructed views in only my mind and capturing snippets of the scenes that passed through the small viewfinder of my camera.

Sensing my enthusiasm and excitement, the pilot, once we arrived at the volcano, hovered the helicopter over the lava flows as I took pictures of the molten red glow that was slowly oozing its way down the mountain over the jagged black lava crust beneath. When we reached the fiery mouth of the volcano, the pilot hovered over its active center as long as possible while I clicked away at the rising steam and fiery furnace. The inner core was similar to the paint pots of Yellowstone National Park that occasionally release fingers of mud into the air as if boiling over. However, instead of being filled with mud, the cauldron of the volcano was filled with molten red ooze, swirling inside as if being stirred by a large, invisible spoon. Through the plumes of smoke and steam, glowing red fingers of molten lava, deep within the volcano's mouth, reached out but could not escape.

As if that wasn't enough, the pilot passed that helicopter over the fiery center multiple times. I knew it was yet another gift as I noticed other tour helicopters in the area. Each flew over the volcano once and was gone.

This experience was not one that could just be tucked away. It was if my whole heart expanded to make room for the gratitude of such an amazing experience. I had always felt close to nature. Now I knew the Earth was a living and breathing entity, and I had had the privilege of seeing her life force.

Back on Oahu: the grand finale
One last scene to my series of Hawaii stories. Back on Oahu. My last week in Hawaii. New Year's Eve. The event: sailing on a catamaran to watch the fireworks. THE New Year's Eve event of Waikiki beach.

I had taken the bus from campus to the beach and roamed the streets looking for the place to buy tickets. After finding the marquee, I followed the sign's arrow to the beach.

I then stood in line like just about everyone else on the island. Except, unbeknownst to me, everyone else in line had already purchased a ticket. There was too much commotion and "buzz" surrounding me to really strike up a conversation with anyone in line. I got as far as confirming that this was the line for sailboat fireworks trip tickets and was ready to camp out.

Almost an hour later, I walked up to the counter window to buy my ticket. The woman behind the counter began to explain that no tickets were available, but then paused and lifted her finger, signaling me to wait as she answered the ringing phone. It was a cancellation call. "You are very lucky," she said. "Someone just canceled."

"Lucky is not the right word," I replied. The woman smiled. I returned a much larger one. I was on the boat. "Maybe I should be buying a lottery ticket instead," I thought to myself as I stepped away from the counter. The way things were going, I would probably win and could buy my own boat… or maybe my own island.

Water skimming the pontoons of the catamaran as it sliced the ocean; laughter; ooh and ahs; and the explosion of colors that filled the sky and seemed close enough to touch—these were added to the amazing treasure box of memories I now carry with me.

This story all started with my first divorce. I have a knowing now. Something that seems "bad" at the time can lead you to something amazing. You just have to be willing to get through the bad to the good that awaits you. I was not completely over Don or my marriage by the end of my month in Hawaii, but I had a glimpse of what the next chapter of my life could become.

Dream big and dare to live it!

recognize the gifts you are given

I have done lots of traveling since my hitchhiking escapade across the United States. Sometimes one trip led to another. One of my trips that led to another began in Central America. It was the second winter after I had moved to Colorado from Michigan. And it was several years after my trip to the Maroon Bells in Aspen, Colorado.

The "official" trip to Central America started out in southern California with a group of friends. From there, we made it as far as Guatemala on many busses—busses that included chickens and pigs. We were heading to Costa Rica, or so we thought. When we heard of shootings in Nicaragua, though, we opted to stop in Guatemala and call it good.

Tom, one of my friends on the Guatemala trip, had spent many years of his life sailing. Tired of busses before we even made it to Guatemala, we opted to go sailing somewhere along the coast of Mexico opposite the Baja peninsula. It turned out that Tom was not the only one with sailing experience. A couple on the boat was from the North Island of New Zealand. They spent most summers sailing in the Bay of Islands, near Auckland, which is where they lived. Apparently the Bay of Islands was a famous area for sailing, but not to me. I had never even heard of New Zealand.

As we were slung out over the boat in our trapezes, Neville and Elaine described the tip of the North Island where the two oceans meet at the end of a place called Ninety Mile Beach, the Fiordland of the South Island and the glaciers and volcanoes in between.

By the end of that day sailing the waters of Mexico, I was more than interested in seeing New Zealand. We exchanged contact information, in case any of us traveled to New Zealand or in case Neville and Elaine ever made it to the States.

New Zealand stayed on my mind during the upcoming summer and beyond. When I spoke of the country, many of my friends seemed interesting in going there...but when it came down to buying a ticket, I realized that if I was going to go, it would be me, myself, and I. I was too excited to go there to let that stop me. Plus, knowing two bodies in a country about the size of Colorado was all I needed. I decided to make my first trip alone to another country.

It was then that the "gifts" started coming my way.

The gift of a discounted ticket
First things first, one late afternoon after work, I stopped at the travel agency closest to my home to inquire about purchasing a plane ticket to New Zealand. After searching for fares, the agent announced a special deal offered by Continental Airlines, which had just started flying there. A trip that normally cost well over a thousand dollars was now under $700. I charged the ticket.

Thanks to the gift of an affordable ticket, my first dot in connecting the dots to get to New Zealand was filled in.

The gift of finance
The next item on my New Zealand to-do list was to find a well-paying job or jobs to pay for that ticket and for my stay, food, and travels. At that time in my life, even a relatively affordable $700 ticket was a substantial expenditure. Since my move to Fort Collins, Colorado, from Detroit, I had worked many jobs, none of which were well paid. The

first was at a photography studio named Mr. Thin Wallet's photography. Although I enjoyed working there, my wallet was also thin. After Mr. Thin Wallet's closed up shop, I worked a variety of waitressing jobs and mowed lawns in the summer.

The job search was the next dot to be connected. I learned from a friend that UPS was hiring people to load trucks for the rush season before the Christmas holidays. The day UPS was accepting applications was a raging blizzard. I didn't own a car at the time, so I walked the several miles in a blizzard, stepped into the temporary UPS office, thawed out my fingers, and filled out the application. The interviewer was so impressed that I had walked there in the snowstorm, he not only hired me on the spot, he also found someone to pick me up for my shifts (which started in the middle of the night) to get me there.

In the wee hours of each morning, I watched many packages travel down the conveyor belt in front of where I stood. My job was to grab only those packages that belonged on my truck and to load them onto the truck by address. It turned out I was so good at this that in less than a month, I was promoted to "runner." As a runner, my job was now in reverse. I rode with the driver in the delivery truck, grabbed packages, and "ran" them to the recipients' doorsteps. Being a runner meant higher pay. The dots were connecting better than I expected.

The gift of a ride to California
Oh and did I mention that my flight to New Zealand left from Los Angeles and that my neighbor who had recently moved in across the street from where I lived in Fort Collins was from La Jolla, California? When I told him of my plans to travel to New Zealand, he offered to drive me to the

airport with a stop to visit his family in La Jolla. Twist my arm. It was my final gift before my trip, and the dots were all connected for getting there.

I left the UPS job just before Christmas with enough money for my New Zealand excursion and then some. My backpack, with enough clothes and camping gear for six weeks (including a single-person tent), and I left for La Jolla and then New Zealand right before the new year.

My plan, in no particular order: To travel to the very northern tip of New Zealand where the two oceans meet, down through the South Island and every national park and beautiful place to see in between. This was another time in my life in which I opted to hitchhike. But as it turned out, I rarely did it, or much of anything, alone. And each person who crossed my path for any length of time had at least one gift to give to me.

The gift of companionship
I met my first set of traveling companions on the plane. It was "back in the day" when you could roam the plane freely during the flight. There was even a lounge. It was there that I met my first pair of newfound friends, one from Australia and one from Canada. The Aussie was a big and burly blond-haired young man who loved to celebrate life. My Canadian friend was slight of build, with short, curly brown hair, a trim beard, and a softspoken manner. We were quite the threesome. While drinking our complimentary champagne to celebrate Continental Airline's first flight to New Zealand, we also decided to toast to New Year's Eve around the world. At each hour, we were certain it would be New Year's Eve somewhere. As we talked between toastings, we also discovered that I had a plan and they didn't. They liked my plan. We decided to begin our travels together.

We spent the first night in modest lodging outside of Auckland to recover from jet lag and our celebration. The next day, our first OMG trip was to Tongariro National Park via Rotorua, the Yellowstone of New Zealand. Unlike Rotorua and its resemblance to Yellowstone, Tongariro was like no place I had ever seen. We had opted for the all-day hike there. In a single day, we wound our way through a trail system of active volcanoes, thermal steam vents, and brilliant emerald and blue lakes, all accompanied by magnificent views in the distance.

It was at one of those magnificent views that I stopped, sat down, and cried. Unbeknownst to my two concerned companions, they were tears of joy. I can't even begin to explain all of the feelings that were released with each tear that flowed so freely. It was as if the floodgates of gratitude and "I can't believe I am in New Zealand" had spilled over. It might have been akin to winning the Publishers Clearing House Sweepstakes, if that ever really even happens.

"Are you all right, mate?" asked the Aussie.

"I am better than all right," I replied. "I just can't believe that I am really here."

They seemed to appreciate my response. At the next magnificent view, they locked their arms together and hoisted me up between them in celebration of making it to the next pass. This time we were celebrating the magnificence of nature at her best, and we were celebrating it together.

The gift of magic
Our next OMG stop was the Waitomo Glowworm Caves. This stop was thanks to my Aussie companion. It had not been on my list. According to the travel brochures, the

glowworm, Arachnocampa luminosa, was unique to New Zealand. The caves were yet another place like no other. I was raised with the summer magic of fireflies. I still miss them to this day. But the glowworms were a different kind of magic. I remember thinking that I was in a planetarium. Instead of billions upon billions of stars, we saw what appeared to be thousands of points of light under a canopy of rock rather than sky.

The gift of courage

My Aussie friend, Jack, and I wanted to backpack through Abel Tasman National Park next. Brian, the Canadian, had decided to head farther south. We exchanged contact information, said our goodbyes to Brian, and headed southwest toward Abel Tasman.

The strip of coast that traces the northern and eastern edges of Abel Tasman National Park is yet one more place like no other. First there were the tides. We were at the mercy of the tides at each pristine beach that filled the spaces between the thick forest and tideline. Thank goodness Jack had brought a tide table of the area with him. And he knew how to read it. If you weren't aware of the timing of the tides, you could end up hiking in the ocean before making it to the other end of a beach.

Then there were the forests. Thick with every living green plant imaginable, or so it seemed, the forests were impassible except for the narrow footpaths. At one point in the hike, even the footpath was gone as we came upon a swinging footbridge high above the forest canopy. Far below, visible through the links of chains and slats of wood, was a narrow ravine, full of crystal-clear water that tumbled down the mossy green valley to the ocean below. It was the far below that was the problem. Even such breathtaking beauty could not assuage my fear of heights. My hands clutched the railings of that bridge, which were much too low for my comfort.

"I am afraid of heights," I admitted.

"What can I do to help you?" Jack responded.

"I just need you to know that," I replied.

What I didn't want him to know was the magnitude of my fears. He knew I was out of my comfort zone, but not that I was petrified. I played the part of someone who could face her fears, calculated our space apart to lessen the bridge's movement, and kept a one-point focus on the backpack in front of me, refusing to look down.

Just having him with me on that bridge made my crossing possible. And I was more than grateful to have made it to the other side.

After our backpacking trip through Abel Tasman, my Aussie traveling companion needed to return home and I needed to head farther south. Christchurch, Milford Sound, Mount Cook, Mount Aspiring, the Routeburn Track and the Milford Track were among the places and hikes left on my self-planned itinerary.

The gift of caring

My first stop on that list was the city of Christchurch. It was here that I learned of the KOA-like camping places that were available. And it was in one of those that my one-person tent became the center of attention. As I sat on the picnic table near my tent, writing postcards, a couple camping nearby stopped by to say "hi" and look more closely at my tent. Others waved from a distance and nodded at my tent.

Even after I climbed inside, a newcomer to the camping area stopped by to "knock" at the head of my tiny tent.

"Are you OK in there?" asked the voice.

I unzipped the mesh netting that covered my head just enough to reach out and lift the flap that served as rain protection. He could hear my response, although I could not see him.

"It is really quite comfortable in here," I assured him.

I felt safe, knowing that others in the campground were looking out for me.

The gift of Stewart Island

Still on the South Island, my next stop was the Milford Track, where I had reserved a four-day hiking slot that included hut accommodations. On this trip, I met a couple who worked in Antarctica, who had about the same hiking pace as I did, and who, like me, were enamored with the bigger than humongous fish that could be seen from the narrow ridge trail that followed the crystal-clear stream far below.

Our conversation eventually shifted from fish to Antarctica. I wanted to know more about what it was like to live there. That conversation began with emperor penguins. They sounded fascinating, but not enough for me to want to go to Antarctica to see them. However, I learned that there were also penguins, much smaller in size, in New Zealand. One of the places they frequented was Stewart Island, just off the bottom tip of the South Island.

I decided I needed to go there.

That night, as if he knew of my plans, a large German fellow wished us all "sweet dreams." Perhaps it was the way he said it. I laughed aloud in response and wished him the same. I had never known that I could feel so comfortable sleeping in a room full of people who were essentially strangers.

The gift of Hawaii

My next traveling companion was also from the States. I met him near Lake Wanaka. I was still on the South Island. We were hitchhiking on opposite sides of the road. I was heading north to Mount Cook and Mount Aspiring to hike and see the glaciers there. He was heading south. Because there was no traffic in either direction, we struck up a conversation. After learning of my plans, he changed directions and joined me. His name was Mike. He had nearly white-blond hair juxtaposed against deeply tanned skin. When we first met, he was wearing a navy-blue-and-white-striped T-shirt that accented his lumberjack body. He seemed like the perfect hiking companion for glacier country. If I fell into a crevasse, I was certain that he could easily pull me out using only one of those arms.

After we explored glacier country, he hiked the Routeburn Track with me. During our time together, it was Mike who told me of Hawaii. He had been before and was going to stop there on the way back to the States. Hawaii was also a place of volcanoes and lush vegetation. Thanks to his descriptions of Hawaii, my one trip leading to another was to continue. Before we needed to part ways, I tried to change my ticket to join him there on my return flight home but could not afford the price of changing my ticket. Instead, Hawaii remained only a stop in the airport and was added to my dream list of places to return. I made it there many years later.

The gift of penguins

After the glaciers and the Routeburn Track, my next memorable stop was Stewart Island. It was home to the penguins I so wanted to see. Here is another "I kid you not" story. As I stepped off the plane and onto the tarmac, I was immediately greeted by two men in a small car, one of whom was drop-dead gorgeous.

"Welcome to Stewart Island!" greeted the gorgeous man. "My name is Jeremy and this is my friend Alex. What brings you to the island?"

"I've come to see penguins," I explained, trying not to stare.

"Penguins? You've come to the right place! I can take you on my boat to see the penguins if you'd like," he continued.

"You have a boat and can take me to see penguins?" I repeated. I was too dumbfounded and excited to even question the safety of a boat ride with two strangers. I really couldn't believe the man attached to those gorgeous blue eyes and striking smile was even remotely interested in giving me the time of day, let alone a boat ride to see "my" penguins.

"Hop in."

"Thank you!" was all I could manage to say.

I slung my backpack into the "boot" of their car and climbed in the back. Minutes later (the drivable portion of the island is short), I stepped into a small speedboat. True to Jeremy's word, as the boat sped out across the ocean, penguins surfaced in the not-too-far distance. I had no idea they were such incredible swimmers, like miniature dolphins leaping out of the water.

"I will take you to a place where you can also see them on land," Jeremy explained.

He moored the boat near one of the beaches of the island. We stepped out and waded in the water to the beach.

It was as if he had sent the penguins an invitation to meet us. As we walked around a corner of the beach, there they were:

a small waddle of penguins standing at attention. As I walked closer, one of them turned to face me and stuck out its flipper as if to shake my hand. They were all so darned cute.

"The outstretched flipper is a warning signal," Jeremy explained. "Don't go any closer."

I felt bad that I had alarmed them. By the end of that afternoon, penguins had moved right up there with dolphins and whales on my attraction scale.

The gift of inspiration

That same day Jeremy also introduced me to fresh mussels. Not my favorite dish, I decided, but the getting them was fun. Afterward, Jeremy, Alex, and I spent time at the lone restaurant bar in the lone town on Stewart Island. Before the evening was over, I asked to be dropped off at the nearest campground. I wanted to hike from there along the coast of the island. Jeremy and I made plans to see each other again before I left the island.

The next morning, although I started off alone on my hike on Steward Island, along the trail I met a freelance journalist who wrote travel articles for a living. Like me, she was also traveling alone. During our hike together, she told me of all the places in the world she had been and how much she enjoyed writing. The passion of her voice and expressions caused me to believe that writing was an integral part of her being. I made a note to check into that option upon my return to the States.

Although I never ended up writing for a travel magazine, that freelance writer's love for her profession inspired me to return to college in the journalism department. Little did I know at that time that writing would become my career of more than 20 years.

The gift of friendship

Before leaving Stewart Island, I spent more time with Jeremy. It was a small island, and he was easy to find. During our time together, I told him of my travels and my life back in the States. He was a veterinarian who kept quite busy despite the small size of the island. I took pictures of him driving his boat so that I could send them as a thank-you gift for his kindness.

Before our time together was over, we exchanged contact information as well as some very memorable kisses. Two days later, my feet barely touched the ground as I boarded the plane to return to the South Island. I was walking on clouds. I'd found penguins, a gorgeous, kind man in a gorgeous country, a romantic encounter that deeply touched my heart, and inspiration for my next career—all in a very short time on a very small island. Who would believe it? Life just doesn't get any better than this, I thought.

The gift of safety

After leaving Stewart Island, I returned to the South Island and headed back toward Auckland. It was during that time that I met my last traveling companion. He was from the eastern foothills of Washington State. By this time, I had already come to the conclusion that anyone I met was for a reason and that the reason would turn out to be a good one. Little did I know I might not have made it out alive from our backpacking trip without him.

We decided to backpack together in Arthur's Pass National Park, not far from where we had met on the road. The highlight of this trip, besides the yet again spectacular scenery, was hiking in on a trail and hiking out without one.

We had slept through the storms of the night inside one of the huts available along the system of trails within the park.

On the hike out, we faced the rushing water of what on our way in had been a much shallower river and attempted to follow the remains of a washed-out trail lined with the trunks of some very large trees.

At one point, crossing that rushing water was the only way out. A seasoned backpacker, my hiking companion instructed me to unbuckle my pack in preparation for the river crossing. We then connected ourselves by holding onto opposite ends of a strap that had been attached to his backpack. By this point, even the swinging bridge of Abel Tasman looked more inviting than what lay before us. During the crossing, we stayed close together. I was hanging tightly to more than the strap when we reached the water that was closing in on my thighs. Although my hiking companion was thin, he was much taller, very strong, and very determined to get us both across that raging river. I was more than happy to comply. If I had thought of it at the time, I would have kissed the muddy gravel that covered the ground on the other side.

The gift of hospitality

My six weeks in New Zealand near an end, the rest of my trip was spent getting back to Auckland and seeing the northern tip of the country via what is known as Ninety Mile Beach. Because I had packed nearly every minute of that trip trying to see every beautiful site there was to see, I was not dropped off at the doorstep of Neville and Elaine's home until the day before my return flight left for the States. I had spent the night before at the home of the Dean of the English Department at Auckland University. His son, who had driven me to his parent's home in what appeared to be a traveling bookmobile, had also offered to take me to Neville and Elaine's home. When I called Neville and Elaine to let them know of my planned arrival, they confirmed their willingness to take me to the airport and expressed their enthusiasm to hear of my travels.

I no longer recall what their house looked like or the exact details of my stay there. What I do recall was their hospitality and warmth. They were pleased that I had such a wonderful trip in their country. And they were all ears to hear of my adventures and shared what they could about the places I missed. I made a point to invite them once again to the States so that I could return their hospitality. Although I never heard from them, I send them warm thoughts often.

The gift of precious memories
Jeremy is another person who has kept a place in my heart. It turned out after I developed the pictures of him and his boat, there was more ocean than boat in the photographs. I framed the one that had the most boat coverage and sent it to him anyway, thinking it's the thought that counts. He was so kind to me.

When Jeremy received the photograph he called me in the States. He definitely had me pegged as a woman of nature. During our conversation he said he had decided that the reason it was more ocean than boat was my love of nature. We both laughed. It sounded much better than admitting my timing had been off when I clicked the shutter of my camera. I had taken many still photos but had never quite gotten the knack of panning to follow a moving subject.

Jeremy asked whether I would return to New Zealand. By this time, I was already accepted into the journalism department at Colorado State University to pursue my dream of writing for a living. I told him of my new path in life and its importance to me. We never spoke again, but the gift of those precious memories lives on in my mind and heart.

Although it was my first trip to another country alone, and, although at the time of my travels, New Zealand was known to have more sheep than people, I was never really alone. Every day of that trip combined to form a chapter in my life full of people who were as wonderful as the country itself. And all because of a couple named Neville and Elaine, whom I met in Mexico and who added New Zealand to my vocabulary and to my list of dreams.

It was in the following of this dream that I learned that even in "alone" times, we are never really alone and that many people who cross our paths do so for a reason. Perhaps it is to receive, give, or exchange a gift we have to offer or are open to receive. I know I received countless gifts during my trip and hope I also touched the lives of those people who were so kind and generous to me.

you are led

It was in the days when camping and campfires went hand-in-hand. A friend and I had hiked to the top of Mt. Whitney. Located outside of Lone Pine, California, it is the tallest peak in the continental United States. And it is spectacular.

At the top, standing in the field of boulders surrounded by patches of snow, I looked out toward the blanket of clouds below us that stretched out as far as the eye could see. I felt on top of the world. Except for the echo of distant conversations of those still making their way up, it was quiet and calm.

Later that day we were just short of collapsed in one of the campgrounds in King's Canyon National Park. Dinner was Jiffy Pop over the campfire. It was dusk by the time we had finished our popcorn dinner. After cleaning up, we stoked the fire. As always, I was mesmerized by the flames, the crackle of burning wood, and the whisper of a breeze that brushed my face as I stared into the fire.

"What a spectacular day! I can't believe we made it up that snowfield without any ice climbing equipment," I remarked. We had been told that the climb was not safe without it. Determined to make it to the top, we left between 2 and 3 a.m. to make it to the top before the snow softened. There were enough tracks to follow that we felt more than safe.

Although worth every tired bone, the hike was arduous, 22 miles roundtrip with an elevation gain of more than 6,000 feet.

By nightfall, I was wiped. The next event for me was going to

the tent to sleep.

"I'm ready to get in the tent and crash," I said to Pam.

The rule between us: The last one to the tent keeps the flashlight. (It was also in the days before headlamps were commonplace.)

"OK," Pam replied. "I'm going to stay up a bit longer. I'll put out the fire."

I left the campfire and walked toward the tent. Pam stayed with the campfire and the flashlight.

I knew the direction of the tent, although I could barely see the ground in front of me and only the black of night ahead. My eyes had become accustomed to staring into the bright light of the campfire.

After only a few steps, I thought I heard a strange, low-pitched, and gruff "bark."

I cautiously asked Pam to shine the flashlight in my direction and toward the tent.

About 30 feet in front of me was over seven feet of brown bear standing upright on two legs, sniffing the air between us. He was standing in front of the door to the tent, which was dwarfed behind him. The bear was facing us but was temporarily blinded by the light.

Without saying a word, I slowly backed up in the direction of Pam's Jeep, which was about ten feet away, in the parking area of our campsite. Pam had followed my lead, keeping the light on the bear the entire time. We climbed into the Jeep and heaved a huge sigh of relief.

"Oh man," Pam managed to say as she switched on the headlights. The bear had dropped to four legs and continued to stare into our headlights. After looking to the left, it finally sauntered off.

"Do you believe that!" I exclaimed. "I am so glad he barked at me. I would have walked right into him. On second thought, I would probably be shredded before I got that close."

"I am not going back out there tonight," declared Pam.

That sounded like a good idea to me as well. However, my five-foot-six body, comprised mostly of legs, could not get comfortable in the front seat of the Jeep. After about 20 minutes, I decided to brave the tent.

Plus, we still needed to put out the campfire.

"I am so tired I just want to be able to lie down flat," I said. "I don't think he will be coming back. I am going in the tent. I'll put out the fire. Just keep the headlights on until I get inside."

I left the safety of the Jeep, doused the fire with our five-gallon water jug, climbed into the tent, and passed out. Pam remained in the Jeep that night. As far as I know that bear never came back.

The thought of what might have happened had I not stopped on the way to the tent is not a pleasant one. This story helps to remind me that I am here for a reason. I have been led, I am led, and I will always be led…as long as I continue to listen.

WHEN YOU FIND YOUR PASSION...

you make things happen

I was moved so deeply, I wanted to dive into the television set and declare, "Take me!" Take me!"

Will Daggett, founder and chairman of the International Center for Leadership in Education, was speaking of the need for junior-high and high-school teachers who have backgrounds in technology. He was addressing a room full of educators during his talk, but it was as if he were addressing me personally. Ten years in the world of computer technology made me more than qualified, or so I thought.

The wheels of the universe were set in motion. Shortly thereafter, I discovered Project Promise—a one-year teaching program targeted at professionals. The program offered the opportunity to teach 5th through 12th grade students in a variety of settings, while also providing courses for me that could lead to a master's degree in education. As a fast-track program targeted at bringing professionals into the teacher community, its goals were in perfect alignment with Will Daggett's vision.

And it was offered at Colorado State University, in Fort Collins, Colorado, where I lived. Perfect!

The program selects 20 students a year. That next year, I was one of them.

To my dismay, despite the fact that I had a degree in technical journalism, I needed a degree in English to teach language arts. I did the only insane thing I could do and crammed most of the required classes into the following summer. You can get lots of credits that way if you don't mind giving up your life to do so. I completed nine credits a month for three four-week sessions—a total of 27 credits. I was on a mission.

My English degree in hand, I left my lucrative position as a technical writer to explore the world of teaching. Unbeknownst to me, I was about to face one of the most gratifying and intense years of my life.

The Project Promise program offered all of its 20 students teaching experience in the mountain town of Leadville, Colorado, and the inner city of Denver. In addition, each of us also had two full-time student-teaching experiences. Mine were in the rural town of Berthoud and in the medium-sized city of Fort Collins.

While at Berthoud High School, I was to teach *Romeo and Juliet* to 9th graders. Having a lifetime of creativity inside me waiting to be released, I decided to begin the unit with masks and the dance scene when Romeo and Juliet meet in Franco Zeffirelli's movie version of *Romeo and Juliet*. After sharing my ideas, I discovered that Jeanne, the teacher there who had so graciously taken me under her wing, was a choreographer. Piece of cake.

Before the unit began, Jeanne's father passed. She would be gone for the duration of the unit.

Determined to carry out my plan anyway, I watched that movie's ballroom scene and practiced in front of my television until I wore out the rewind button on the remote.

The dance was simple, really, but to someone who had never taught dancing, who never had or raised children, and who was now facing for the first time the responsibility of teaching more than 30 14-year-olds, the dance and the unit felt anything but simple. Luckily, I was more excited than nervous. "How could it be anything but fun?" remained the focus of my thoughts. And the unit was based on experiential learning activities that I hoped the students would not quickly forget.

Mask day and the opening day of the unit, I arrived with a bag of undecorated but shiny silver, gold, red, and green masks that I had purchased at a local costume store. Feathers, glitter, ribbon, lace, fabric, trim, sequins, construction paper, and beads of many colors as well as bottles of Elmer's glue filled another bag. That class period was spent adding these sundry decorations to each mask underneath.

I cannot recall each individual mask, but I do recall being deeply touched by the activity. Even as a not-yet-real teacher, I was able to tell when a student gave his or her best effort. No matter the mask, whether dark in nature, glamorous, or comic, each was a tribute to student effort at its best.

Dance day, I arrived in a green velvet full-length gown that was meant to help me appear as if I had just walked off the set of Franco's movie. It was borrowed from the local theater, thanks to a friend who was an actor there. The students donned their masks, as did I.

When it was time for my demonstration with a partner, to my delight and relief, more than one male hand flew into the air. Here is how it went: Bow to the person across from you. Walk forward two steps. Walk back two steps. Raised right hands touch across. Raised left hands touch across. Raised right arms cross each other. Raised left arms cross each other. Back two steps. Forward two steps. Lock raised arms, spin around and switch to the opposite line. Raise both arms at the elbow. Face away from the person across. Move down one person in line. Turn to face your new partner, and repeat the sequence.

After the demonstration, the students formed two lines facing each other. Each girl was across from a boy, with a boy on each side of her. I am not sure the numbers were even, but it all worked out.

We practiced without music first, then I turned on the music. By the end of the song, the class moved as one unit. Looking down the lines of student faces I saw a mixture of intent concentration and smiles. All were engaged. I had been in the Project Promise program long enough to know that in the world of high school, that is a sign of success.

When the dance was over, the students returned to their seats to begin their research project on a topic of their choice related to the times in which the play was set. Examples included fashion, health care, family life, education, sports, recreation, the arts, and government. But now each student had experienced what it was like to dance in those times and wear masks, a practice common to that period. The room was abuzz with enthusiastic and focused activity. Once again, I didn't need years of teaching experience to realize that this was every teacher's dream, at least for teachers who dream of their students and classrooms.

Later, when it was time to present their research projects, many students continued the theme and wore clothing of the times.

Passion, passion, passion was rewarded with student success, success, and more success.

Tears, smiles, and many thank yous later, I went on to my next assignment, Preston Junior High.

you lose the fear

You would think that teaching a roomful of more than 30 12-year-olds would be challenge enough. But not for me. I had another idea, and I was determined to see it through.

The unit: Sensory writing. The school: Preston Junior High. The idea: Setting up sensory stations around the room, each displaying one type of object. So that it was truly a sensory experience, the objects would be of different shapes, textures, colors, and sizes. Item ideas included stuffed animals, iridescent glowsticks, different colors and textures of yarn, cotton balls, yo-yos, feathers, and a live snake.

Why the idea of a snake crept into one of my lesson plans is a question that remains unanswered. What I do know is that after I started Project Promise, ideas for lesson plans came to me day and night. Once in my mind, no matter how elaborate or unusual the idea, I felt the need to bring it to fruition.

I have had a fear of snakes since childhood. Who knows where such fears come from, as no snake has ever done me harm. Perhaps it is just that I prefer warm, fuzzy creatures with cute faces. Or perhaps I need to know where a creature has gone and whether it is coming back. It's hard to tell about such things when snakes are involved.

When I lived in Michigan, I would occasionally see garter snakes. Seeing them slither away in the grass always left me with the heebie jeebies.

Weighing my dilemma—on the one hand, a fear of snakes;

on the other, what might be a once-in-a-lifetime opportunity for students to handle a snake up close and personal and oh what a sensory experience—the students won out. My fear of snakes would just have to be overcome. Besides, the science teacher down the hall had a pet boa constrictor.

The day the sensory writing unit began, multiple stations were set up around the room. A big, brown, soft, and fuzzy stuffed Tasmanian Devil; iridescent pink, green, and orange glowsticks; a silver metal Slinky; cotton balls; yo-yos (both plastic and wooden); an assortment of feathers; and a troll doll with a dark olive body and lime green hair were among the items on display.

One of the sensory stations was mobile. It was me, draped in Mr. Prebble's snake. Well, actually, the snake was draped down one clothed arm. Luckily for me, the snake had been recently fed and was, thank goodness, quite docile and content to lie down my arm, where all three feet of him had been carefully placed by the science teacher who owned him. I held my right arm raised at the elbow so the snake could rest his head there. Anytime I rearranged him, his light- and dark-brown patterned skin was smooth and warm, unlike my scaly and cold-to-the-touch misperception.

Student reactions were mixed. Some students were excited, some knew all about snakes, and some were quite frightened. All were surprised to see me wearing Mr. Prebble's snake.

To keep my fear in check, I stayed focused on the students who came by the optional station to see and touch the snake. Near the end of the time period, one student who had been watching from a distance walked up.

"I am afraid of snakes, but I want to touch it," she declared.

She kept her distance, her eyes wide. "Is it cold and slimy?"

"No, actually he is smooth and warm. You should touch him and see for yourself," I coaxed.

Coming closer and reaching out her hand, she lightly ran her fingers over the skin of its body. "Oh my gosh! It doesn't feel anything like I thought it would!" she exclaimed. Her face lit up with a look of triumph.

How could I even think of being afraid after that?

If nothing else was accomplished that day, my snake station was well worth the initial uneasiness of wearing a three-foot snake. At least one student could write not only about the feel of a snake's skin but of moving past her fears to actually touch one. What an accomplishment!

In hindsight, if I had really thought about my fears beforehand, I might have broken into a cold sweat...or at least decided to leave out the snake. I can't really explain why that snake was so important. Perhaps it was just enough to know even for that hour, when you follow your passion, you leave fear behind. And sometimes your passion enables others to do the same.

your heart knows what to do

One of my favorite nonfiction book series is by David Feldman. His "Imponderables" books, which I owned and used in my classroom, include *Do Penguins Have Knees?*, *What are Hyenas Laughing at, Anyway?*, *Why Do Clocks Run Clockwise?* and *When Do Fish Sleep?*

My question to ponder is: Where do ideas come from? In fact, where did David Feldman and his followers get ideas for enough imponderable questions to fill so many books?

I still cannot answer those questions, but this story helps to illustrate the fact that when your intention is from the heart, the ideas you need will come to you.

I used to do some kind of volunteer work at least once a year. Some commitments lasted longer than others. Over the years, they included being a mentor to at-risk youth, writing a newsletter for a wilderness volunteer group, assisting with local running races, and coaching cross-country running. Volunteering to work with children was my favorite. Perhaps because I never had children of my own, youth hold a special place in my heart.

It was spring, the year after I had coached cross-country for a local junior-high school. This time, I assisted the track-and-field coaches for Special Olympics. We met every Saturday morning.

My first morning, a handful of youth ranging in ages from about eight to 13 were on the track. We began with introductions, including to the parents who had accompanied their sons and daughters.

During the warm-up, I ran with the youngest runner's little brother. He was all enthusiasm, but he wasn't old enough to participate in Special Olympics. We laughed and talked and "raced" until we ran our lap.

When it was time for the real practice, the coaches explained the instructions for the first run, and the assistants (that included me) ran alongside the youth to support them and keep them on task.

One of the older girls stayed close to me. Every inch of her tall, lank body was ready to run. We became running partners. Each time the young girl had to run without the assistants (as if in a race), I stood at the finish line as her cheerleader. Although she didn't always stay in her lane, the eyes behind her glasses stayed focused on the finish line.

While spending most of my time as the young girl's support system, I noticed the youngest boy, who was not as enthusiastic about running as my running partner. He had short-cropped brown hair and a look of consternation when he ran. I am not sure he had bought into the idea of running or at least not for the duration of each running practice.

His running technique, if you could call it that, included running with his hands in his pockets.

Mind you, it wasn't a big deal how or where the children ran as long as they were there and trying. But perhaps subconsciously I was concerned about the young boy's balance and whether he might more easily take a tumble if his hands were tucked away. No matter. After that practice, an idea came to me when I didn't even know I was trying to come up with one.

My car and I were headed for home. About a block down the road, the idea of looking for a finger puppet entered my conscious thoughts.

What a great idea! I thought. How the heck did I even think of such a thing? was my next thought.

I headed to a local toy store to look for finger puppets. Sure enough, the toy store in Old Town Fort Collins had lots of them. I bought two—one for the boy and one for his younger brother, both the same. Tan, furry rabbits with long, floppy ears seemed to be the appropriate shape. Two of the same kind seemed the safest choice. I didn't want the younger brother to feel left out, and I didn't want either of them thinking the other got a "better" puppet.

When I arrived at practice the next Saturday, I kept the puppets hidden in my jacket pocket. I called the parents aside first to get their approval.

"Yes. Let's try it," was their response.

I approached the youngest runner. "I got you something," I said. "And I got something for you too," I said to his brother, who was also standing beside me.

I handed each of them a puppet.

They each smiled in response.

"It's a rabbit," said the young runner, stroking the brown fur and long, droopy ears.

"Mine is a hamster," said the younger brother, raising it in the air.

It worked. All smiles, the older brother headed to the track. He ran each lap with his finger puppet and both hands out of his pockets. His arms swung freely and his legs stretched out farther with each running step.

The boy wore his puppet for the duration of that practice,

including for the other field activities, even long-distance jumping and the discus throw. He also brought it to every practice thereafter.

Ever since my teaching experience, when my lesson-plan ideas were nearly nonstop, I have wondered where ideas come from, especially the ones that you didn't realize you were even trying to think of. Since my experience with the Special Olympians, I believe that we have extra help with ideas when our intention comes from the heart. Perhaps with the help of our heart, we are more open to receiving them. I had compassion for that boy and all of the youth at practice. They were such bright lights of enthusiasm and determination. The young boy turned out to be just as enthusiastic and determined; he just needed a "buddy" to run with and carry along.

Not only where ideas come from but also how we find what we need to bring them to fruition is a thought to ponder. I have frequented that children's store in Old Town Fort Collins over the years since that spring and have never seen the finger-puppet rack there again.

WHEN YOU ARE GENEROUS...

for you

others are generous in turn

My running shoes had reached their 100-mile usage mark. It was time for new ones. I headed to my favorite running store.

It was early Friday evening after work.

When I arrived at the store, a couple was also there shopping for shoes and running clothes for someone who appeared to be their son.

Walking past them, I found the latest pair of Nike's in the same style as the ones I was replacing. They had my size. They fit. My running-shoes mission was accomplished. I decided my next mission was to check out the running clothes. I found two sleeveless running tops and a pair of capri running tights.

While I was at the register ready to pay for my purchases, the man who was shopping with his wife and son noticed my armful of clothes.

"Would you like a 20-percent-off coupon for those running clothes?" he offered.

"Don't you need the coupon for your son?" I asked.

"We have an extra," he responded.

"In that case, yes, I can use it. Thank you so much! Perhaps I will see you again to pay it forward."

"Not likely," he responded.

"Well, we will just have to see, won't we?" I replied, smiling.

The next day, the thought came to me that I should have

given them the two free passes to my health club that I had received from the membership office the week before.

Two days later, the same gentleman approached me as I was doing crunches on the mat at that very health club. I smiled in recognition. Offering him free passes to the health club to which he already belonged wouldn't have worked.

"You won't believe what happened!" he exclaimed, grinning. "The day after we gave you the coupon, we were at Arby's. The person ahead of us in line offered us a coupon for Arby's. Do you believe that?"

"Wow! That got paid forward really quickly. I'm glad I saw you again to hear about it," I added.

He smiled.

Talk about synchronicity and paying it forward. To keep the momentum going, I gave the health club passes to a friend the next day.

WHEN SOMETHING NEEDS TO HAPPEN...

you have more help than you can ever imagine

Some things in life just need to happen. I am certain this was the case with the first fundraiser I planned and created from start to finish.

It was named "Movin' on Up with the Matthews House." It was to benefit at-risk youth from the Matthews House—an organization that empowers young adults in transition to navigate difficulties on the road to self-sufficiency. Many of the young people in the program are or have been part of foster care, the justice system, or both. Many have also lived in generational poverty. The Matthews house goals include helping these youth acquire the skills necessary for living independently, including obtaining and retaining a job, solving problems, managing money, and building solid relationships.

The fundraiser's main goal was to outfit a handful of Matthews House youth with job-interview clothes matched to their professional aspirations and selected with the assistance of Colorado State University (CSU) fashion design students. The event was to include a fashion show in which the youth would model the clothes for which money was being raised.

The spark of inspiration
Although I didn't know it at the time, the idea for the fundraiser started with a spark of inspiration: a trip to a leather factory in northern Turkey.

I traveled to Turkey in the fall of 2011 with a group of

friends I consider "family." We had just finished touring one of the many historical sites there. The leather factory was a late-afternoon stop on the way back to our hotel.

We arrived at a warehouse full of luxurious leather coats, jackets, and bags. With only a glimpse of the racks of leather clothing, we were escorted to the back of the warehouse for a fashion show preview of some of the jackets and coats available.

I had barely found a seat when I was selected from the crowd to participate in the fashion show. The sales clerks probably saw dollar signs coming out of my eyes as I entered the store. I am sure they decided in unison: "Got one." In any event, although I had modeled once in my youth, this was different. It was a pretty amazing experience, one I will not forget.

I was escorted with two other "volunteer" models from our group to yet another back room, where we were instructed to select two leather jackets or coats. I chose a short, dark brown leather jacket and a longer, dark brown leather coat that included a hood trimmed with lighter brown fur.

On cue, I walked down the aisle, blinded by the bright lights and wrapped in a jacket that fit like a glove and felt as soft as silk. I was escorted on either side by two male models. As we strutted arm-in-arm, I am certain my smile was as bright as those lights. For that instant my feet barely touched the ground. I could have been on assignment on a runway in Manhattan. Coat number two was even more high-end than the jacket. And round two on the runway was just as much fun. This time, Hollywood crossed my mind. I was ready to act the part of someone surrounded in luxury on a daily basis.

That initial transformation in my attitude was only the

beginning. Once in the warehouse, I spent the first few minutes only scanning the racks and running my hands over the different textures of leather. I was drawn to the ones that felt like silk, although I also envisioned myself surrounded by leather edged in fur, if only for that afternoon.

The second transformation happened when I slipped on the jacket that I ended up purchasing. It was not only as soft as silk, it was reversible—light tan on one side and on the other, a design with the coloring of leopard skin but the pattern of brushstrokes. The jacket felt so good against my skin that I looked in the mirror and hugged myself. I was styling. Since I was already spending more money on a jacket that I had ever spent on a jacket in my life, I decided to do the same for a matching leather purse. Sign me up, Hollywood.

That afternoon in the Turkish leather factory, I experienced the transformation of making something mine I used to think was unattainable and of experiencing the feelings that went with such an upgrade.

The rest of the ingredients
And although I describe the spark of inspiration as starting in Turkey, I wonder whether much of my life led up to the Matthew's House fundraiser.

First of all, I (usually) have a zest for life that is contagious. I developed my enthusiasm after losing a close friend at a young age. We went to high school together, traveled to Toronto together to celebrate our full-ride college scholarships, and started college together.

Katie died of a brain tumor shortly after she started college. But before she died, she spent several weeks in the hospital, where I visited her regularly. One day as I sat next to her hospital bed and held her hand, she cried out.

"I want to finish school and travel the world!" she explained between her tears.

I felt like someone was reaching into my chest and yanking out my heart.

My last visit, the nurse said that Katie was unconscious and would not know I was with her. But after the nurse left the room, I reached for Katie's hand. She squeezed it. A lone tear rolled down her right check. Many more tears rolled down both of mine. The next day, Katie left this world.

Perhaps since then I have been trying to live for both of us. In any event, as anyone who has been involved in fundraisers knows, you need enthusiasm and a strong belief in what you are doing to "rally the troops" behind you.

I also feel an affinity for youth who are faced with adult circumstances and responsibilities at a young age. Although I lived at home until the age of 18 and had been raised in a loving family, I was ready to leave much sooner. I simply wanted the freedom of independence. It was only my father's request that I stay at home to help out my mom that kept me there.

Having been married to an adrenaline junkie, I also understand the courage required to take risks—a courage that doesn't always come easy.

Putting together my zest for life, my affinity for young people, and my willingness to take worthwhile risks, I knew I wanted to help at-risk youth, and after visiting the website, I knew I wanted it to be the Matthews House. Thank goodness they were willing to take a risk with me and supported my efforts.

Here is my short list of additional qualifications:

- I am fearless when it comes to asking for help for others in need.

- I know a lot of wonderful and generous people, to whom I am continually grateful.

- Those people also knew people who offered to help.

- I just plain love clothes.

So there you have it—all the ingredients for a fundraiser that would include a fashion show. Oh, and throw in new "dos" for the Matthews House "models," donated by a local hair stylist.

The event

The fundraiser brought together many things: donations and assistance from several local women's clothing stores and one shoe store; cooperation from Matthews House employees, including the director; Matthews House youth who were looking for jobs; assistance from CSU fashion design students; a hip-hop performance and lessons by a professional dance group; a hip-hop performance by the Matthews House youth; a reporter and photographer from our local newspaper; countless hours donated by an amazing graphic artist; generosity beyond measure; and a packed house in the ballroom above the Rio Grande restaurant in Fort Collins, Colorado.

I am not sure I can ever explain how it all came together. What transpired was the "movin' on up" of an amazing number of people.

Unfortunately, shortly before event time, there were also some not-so-amazing, last-minute challenges. The day before the event I learned that one of the at-risk youth who was to be in the fashion show was sick and would not be able to attend. When you only have five models, one missing model is not a good thing. Since I was heading home from work when I received the phone call, I detoured to the shop that was holding her outfits. Miraculously, I was the same size. Piece of cake. I would be her stand in.

The second phone call came the night of the event as I was walking to the venue with an armful of the professional clothes we were hoping to be able to purchase. The woman who was to emcee the fashion show part of the event had just lost her husband to a brain aneurysm. After reeling from the shock of that news and asking the person who called to pass on my condolences, I dialed the first CSU fashion design student cell phone number on my list.

"Are you willing to emcee the fashion show?" I asked. "I have index cards with the information you would read for each youth."

She was hesitant, but she offered for all of the fashion design students to emcee as a group. Perfect! I thought.

Luckily, thanks to one of the local shop owners, I had gifts for each of them. After hanging up the outfits in the back room and passing out the gifts to each student to thank them for all of their help, the Matthews House youth models arrived. It was time for the fashion-show rehearsal.

As my handful of friends arrived to help set up the ticket table, silent auction, desserts, and the event programs, I was being coached by one of the fashion design students with modeling experience on how to model for the fashion show routine. After two runway rehearsals, the assistant sales clerk for the original woman who was to be the emcee arrived. It turned out that Amber was also the same size as the model who couldn't attend. And oh, by the way, she had modeling experience. She graciously offered to take my place. Things were looking up!

The hip-hop dancers had also arrived and the sound system was working. I ran through the program with them as well as the Matthews House youth who would also be performing a hip-hop routine.

As I walked towards the front of the room to start the event, I glanced at the display of food. It was lovely. It included an assortment of appetizers provided by the Rio Grande as well as a display of luscious and lovely homemade desserts that a friend and her daughter had spent at least one entire evening making. The event had not even really begun and already I was moved beyond measure. I gave my friend Linda and her daughter Elizabeth a thumbs up as I passed the dessert table.

By 7 p.m. I was standing at the podium and staring out at a packed house buzzing with conversation and laughter.

After tapping the microphone to get everyone's attention, I was on. The event began with introductions and a welcome by the Matthews House director, followed by a moving speech and success story by a Matthews House "graduate."

Next was the performance by the local hip-hop dance troupe, followed by a hip-hop dance lesson. During this time, Amber discreetly informed me that I was still wearing the camisole top that was part of her fashion show outfit. Although I missed part of the hip-hopping, I was able to change clothes well before the fashion show needed to begin.

After the dance lesson, I was back at the podium (minus the camisole). It was time for more introductions and the fashion show. Each CSU fashion design student introduced one of the models. The announcements included the aspirational job, interests, background, and information about the outfit of each Matthews House youth as she walked out onto the imaginary runway in the midst of tables where the attendees were seated and standing.

By this time a reporter from the local newspaper had also arrived in response to my request and a professionally written, donated press release.

Each girl was all smiles and did a superb job of modeling her outfit. Recalling my experience in Turkey, I could relate to the look in their eyes, the way they carried themselves down the catwalk, and their smiles. They had the "attitude" required for "movin' on up" to new heights.

During an intermission and interview questions by the reporter came the last call for silent-auction bids. Yet another local store had donated handbags with "surprise" jewelry inside each. Donated jewelry and clothes from local clothing shops were also open for bidding.

After the silent auction bidding closed, another set of Matthews House youth performed a hip-hop routine that was deserving of the standing ovation it received.

For more audience participation, as the silent auction winners were announced, each "winner" came up front to model their purchase.

Soon it was time for thank yous, clean up, and money counting. Had we raised enough money to pay for the career outfits for the five Matthews House youth?

Thanks to the friends who helped me (including one friend who singlehandedly sold two tables' worth of tickets), the Matthews House youth and a friend who volunteered to help with ticket sales, the hip-hop performers, the four clothing stores owners and shoe store owner who participated and donated silent auction items, the shop owner who came up with the name for the event, and the generosity of those who attended, we raised more than enough money to cover event expenses and not one but two outfits for each of the five youths who participated in the fashion show.

All the planning in the world couldn't have prevented the last-minute mishaps. Yet, it all worked out and was an amazing success.

I saw many transformations that evening, and not just of the Matthews House youth who participated in the fashion show. The event had touched the lives of many people that night, including those who really heard the stories of these youth and of the Matthews House organization. Even the audience members who participated in their first time hip-hop dance lesson left with a livelier step and a new experience under their belts. I also learned later that the event made it to YouTube and was the "hot topic" at the Matthews House for weeks after.

I know I am a different person thanks to that event. I also know that I had more than a village behind me on this one and that I was helped every step of the way.

WHEN YOU LOSE SOMEONE

YOU CARE FOR...

keep an open mind

Shortly before writing this book, I lost my favorite pair of earrings. I had the white pearls when I arrived at the health club and left without them. When I realized they were missing, I checked with the front desk and carefully scoured the parking lot on my route to the car before heading home. No dice.

That evening when I changed clothes, I found one of them resting on my collarbone. Thinking its mate may have also been hiding on my person somewhere, I then searched every inch of the room, including my dresser, the floor of the room, the floor under the dresser, my car, my clothes, and the path between the garage, my house, and my room. Again, no dice. Packrat that I am, I laid the one I'd found on the right-hand side of my dresser, next to my jewelry box, just in case the other turned up. The single white pearl continued to draw my attention in the days that followed as it lay alone in the otherwise empty space on my dresser.

Two weeks later, I stopped looking for the missing earring and bought a replacement pair. I placed the new pair on my dresser alongside the lone earring.

A few days later, I lost something truly important. A friend.

The text from a mutual friend said to call as soon as possible. I called. The news: A fluke that had started in the hospital ended in death. My friend Rosalie had an anaphylactic reaction to the medication she'd been given to treat a flare-up of bronchitis.

127

Rosalie was among a set of friend I consider family. I had known her for about five years. She was a gifted healer who, among other things, helped others to identify areas in which they might be "stuck" so they could continue to move forward in life. I would see her at yearly gatherings and would call her occasionally in Albuquerque, New Mexico, where she lived. Each time I saw her in person, she always remembered the news I had mentioned when we last talked on the phone.

The morning after I learned of Rosalie's passing, I was just about ready to head to work. I wore my new pearl earrings daily, but I had not yet put them on. I opened the door to my dressing room and reached over to my dresser to grab the earrings. I looked down and thought I saw four earrings where only three should have been. I did a double take and looked again. The lost earring lay next to the other three as plain as day. I gently lifted the earrings off the dresser to make sure they were real.

I have lost track of things before. I call them senior moments. But the missing earring was not a senior moment. It had vanished one day and reappeared weeks later.

My first thought was to check in with the intuitive I had spoken with a few days before. She had mentioned that what appeared to be unusual things might happen in the few days following our session.

I sent the intuitive an email asking her about the disappearance and reappearance of the earring. I did not mention the loss of my friend, only the mysterious return of my earring. Here is what I wrote:

> You mentioned that things might happen within these few days following my appointment.

One thing I noticed is that material things that I thought I lost have "come back." The most interesting was a pearl earring that I just loved. I had one of them, but had looked EVERY-WHERE for the other. I had finally given up and bought another pair. I assumed I had lost the other at the gym (long story). This morning the missing earring showed up on my dresser like it had always been there (although I can guarantee you it had not :-)).

If you can shed any insight into the message for this one, let me know.

And here was her reply:

No problem. I love follow-up questions that relate to unexplained, good things happening! Did the earrings mean anything to you regarding someone else? It was an "I am here for you" message. It could just be your guides, but feels like someone who has passed on.

The earring's return is something I cannot logically explain to this day. But isn't it comforting to think that perhaps when friends or loved ones leave this Earth, the possibility of connection remains?

know that all is well

I have one more story of death. Once again, I lost a friend who was family.

This time the call came when I was at work. I was shocked and dismayed. Gloria wasn't supposed to die.

But she had died, of a heart condition in the early hours of a Friday morning. Right before she passed, she had called her daughter in Denver, who called her grandson in Fort Collins. She passed shortly after that call.

She had lived all her just-shy-of-86 years to the fullest. Like my friend Rosalie, Gloria was also a healer, administering homeopathic health care to alleviate allergy-based problems and body imbalances. She was also a noted speaker at international healthcare events.

I had known Gloria for almost as long as I lived in Fort Collins. I met her through her daughter, who was also a friend and a coworker during the beginnings of my technical writing career. We are still friends to this day.

After I received the call, I did what I often do when faced with bad news: I got moving. That day after work, I drove home, got on my bike and rode toward Lory State Park. It was the park I had frequented when I lived in the foothills, and it was a bike ride I took almost weekly in the summer.

It was a warm afternoon in late July. The hillsides were still green and lush, despite the heat. A warm breeze brushed against my face as I headed west and then south along the foothills. The air smelled of horses, which were quietly grazing in the pastures on both sides of the road.

By the time I reached the edge of the foothills, I was more into my head than the scenery. I was having quite the conversation with myself along the way.

"Why did she leave?" I asked the wind. Gloria had just returned from a trip to Montana. I had heard wonderful things about her trip—how she had gone horseback riding and how well she had ridden. She had even tried her hand at horse polo there.

Unfortunately, no answers to that question came. So I asked Gloria, "Please give me a sign that all is well."

After asking the question, I looked up from the road. I was passing the familiar peacock farm on the right, just before the last turn to Lory State Park. My answer: At that very moment, in the wire pen in which a handful of peacocks were standing, the only pure-white peacock lifted and fanned its tail feathers, waving its plumage front to back as if to say hello. The fan appeared nearly translucent, with brighter spots of white that shimmered and traced the lines of each feather.

At almost the same instant, the peacock cried out in the high-pitched, shrill, repetitive call that only peacocks can make.

I knew it was a sign from Gloria. Not only had I just asked her for a sign, I had passed that farm nearly every week for years and had never once heard the peacocks there or noticed the white one. What's more, white was the color of Gloria's hair and of her favorite horse at the Montana ranch from which she had just returned.

I stopped in appreciation, smiled, turned back, and headed home.

Whatever it takes to let me know all is well. Thank you, Gloria.

WHEN YOU THINK YOU HAVE
REACHED YOUR LIMITS...

think again

I have chosen this as my last story because, for me, athletic endeavors that push you beyond your normal limits are a good analogy for life. I now firmly believe that you are never given more than you can handle in life. I say this only because I have sworn otherwise more than once, but here I am.

I have been a wanna-be athlete since I earned my Red Card. To earn that card, I took a weeklong firefighting training course and passed the physical step test, but not the running test. At the time, I only needed to pass one of them, not both. Getting my Red Card meant I was a full-fledged volunteer firefighter. It also meant I was on the road to a new level of fitness.

From then until now, I am sure I have run thousands of miles, including one marathon. (That running test was a LONG time ago.)

To me, "athlete" is a relative term. I know two Olympic runners and rode Ride the Rockies with three bicycle racers. Let's just say I completed the 100-mile day of that bike trip in eight hours. Everyone else I knew took under five. I am probably more tenacious than fit.

As a runner I have learned that, as in life, some days are better than others. While hanging out with some serious athletes, I also learned the meaning of hitting a wall. The lesson is that you can hit a wall and somehow, miraculously, bounce back. And sometimes, as in life, all it takes is someone to be there for you.

The day of my one and only marathon was not a good one for me. I do not recall how many walls I hit running that day. I know there were at least two. The main thing I remember is the friend who came out to run the last mile with me and cheer me on.

The race started 26 miles outside of Steamboat Springs, Colorado, in Hahn's Peak Village, which is at about 8,100 feet in elevation. The race ends in front of the courthouse in the middle of Steamboat Springs, which is at about 6,700 feet elevation. Although overall the race is downhill, there are many rolling hills along the way, including a steep and significant incline at mile 21.

It was a beautiful day, and I had started out strong. The course follows a paved county road along the Elk River Valley. The scenery, when I was able to focus on it, was spectacular—a lush green valley and snow-kissed mountain peaks.

I hit my first wall after mile 13. I grabbed a pack of gel I was carrying in my jacket pocket and made sure to drink more water. At that point the fluids and the energy gel kept me going. I tried desperately to focus on the scenery.

I hit another wall at about mile 21, when the steep incline began. That wall seemed never-ending and lasted until nearly the finish line. I thought of a friend who had run the New York City marathon. She ended up taking the subway to the finish line. No subway here, I thought. I could run or walk, but I needed to keep going. I chose to attempt to continue to run.

My next thought was the one I used in training. You can always go just one more mile, I would tell my friend as we ran laps at the track. Today, it was what I kept telling myself.

By the time I was to mile 25, my head and body were tilted

to one side, and I am sure my face wore a look of agony. I only had a little over one more mile to go, but I so wished I was done. The last mile was also uphill. My legs felt like lead weights. As I was trying to think of anything other than body parts, I heard someone calling my name.

"Go, Carole!"

It was my friend Michelle, and she was running up to me and then running beside me.

"You can do it, Carole!" she cheered.

It was her mantra and mine for that last mile. For all I know, I might have even picked up the pace with Michelle cheering me on. What I do know for a fact is that I finished.

When you think you have reached a limit, physical or otherwise, perhaps you have more strength than you think. And when you need help the most, someone often shows up.

acknowledgments

First and foremost, I am deeply grateful to Sharon O'Hara, my guide and teacher who has lit my path through what feels like so many lifetimes within this one. With Sharon's assistance and teachings, I have built the foundation that has enabled me to expand my awareness to see the symbols and messages with which we are presented throughout our lives and to be aware of the assistance that is ours for the asking.

Next, a fond thank you to my Growing Place family, who, simply in the knowing they are available, help me to keep on keeping on in the face of adversity.

With much love, I am forever grateful to my mother, Emily Choike, who modeled the epitome of relentless devotion, whether I paid attention or not.

A special thanks to my dear friends Kristin Mouton, Denise Padilla, Linda Palmieri, Shelby Kahl, and Linda Ripley, for their patience, support, and ideas in the bringing of this book to fruition. I can't even begin to count the emails that I sent asking for opinions on most every aspect of the book, often more than once. You are some of the most wonderful friends on the face of this planet.

In recognition of another set of special people in my life, who didn't get quite as many emails as the previous list but of whom I am much appreciative as well, thanks to Susan Kordis, Sue Gallup, Pam Sullivan, Claire Mouton, and Martha Tipton for their feedback, ideas, and encouragement. An additional thanks to Susan Kordis for her assistance with my bio.

It is with humble appreciation that I send my gratitude to Teresa Espaniola, who gifted me a draft of a cover design that was to eventually become the basis of the design for the final cover. My heart is still touched by her generosity and talent.

My deep appreciation and thanks to Karla Oceanak, my writing coach and editor, as well as to Launie Parry, the graphic artist with limitless creativity who not only made this book a reality, but the making of it fun!

Thank you to the talented staff of Harper Point Photography, who produced my portraits for the book, including Caleb Young, the photographer, Michael Douglas, photo editor, and Kira Friedman, who patiently assisted me in selecting the photographs.

I also send a heartfelt thanks to Lynnie Long, who brought Thor and his many lessons into my life. Thanks also to Shannon Ricciardi and her family as well as to Stephanie and John McCormick for providing Thor with such loving homes.

To my ever-so-thoughtful friends Teresa and Randy Redmond-Ott, Cynthia Donovan, and Erica Marjoram, who gave me the momentum and support I needed as I settled into my new post-divorce life.

Thanks also to my longtime friends Greg Duff and Gary McDonald, as well as to all of the people I met in my cross-country travels who helped make my Maroon Bells dream (and then some) a reality.

Thanks to the travelers and residents of New Zealand who touched my life.

A special thanks to Dr. Robert Richburg and the rest of the Project Promise staff for assisting me in realizing my dream of becoming a teacher. Thanks also to the master teachers Marty Marsh, Nancy Tellez, and Jeanne Wade, who served as my mentors, laying the foundation for my teaching career. And not to be forgotten, my gratitude to the students of Berthoud High School and Preston Junior High for their engagement in my classroom activities.

The list of generous and caring individuals who assisted with the Matthews House fundraiser would fill a book in itself. Please know that even though everyone is not mentioned here, I thank and appreciate each and every one of you! My deep appreciation to the Matthews House staff, especially Carolyn Davis and Joyce Dickens, who took a risk to support me in bringing the Matthews House fundraiser to fruition. I am also eternally grateful to the store owners whose generosity, caring, and support helped to make the Matthews House fundraiser a reality and success, including Kristin Mouton, owner of Rain Boutique, Meriam Hanson, owner of Cira, Jillian Grenrood, owner of Sole Mates, and Avriel Agnello, former owner of Biyazzi.

And finally, to everyone who has chosen to read this book, I sincerely hope it touches your life and propels you forward in fulfilling your dreams, following your passions, and recognizing the extraordinary in what appear to be the ordinary events in your lives.

Warmly,
Carole Balawender

now it's your turn

Carole invites you to share your own stories of
finding the extraordinary in the ordinary on the
Just Stories Facebook page! No matter how simple,
your stories have meaning and need to be told.
When we help each other learn to live with
wonder, life becomes, well, pretty wonderful.

facebook.com/pages/Just-Stories

Made in the USA
Monee, IL
07 April 2023